THE CHANGE LEADER

Using A Gestalt Approach with Work Groups

H.B. Karp, Ph.D.

Jossey-Bass
Pfeiffer

San Francisco

Jossey-Bass Pfeiffer

350 Sansome Street, 5th Floor
San Francisco, California 94104-1342
(415) 433-1740; Fax (415) 433-0499
(800) 274-4434; Fax (800) 569-0443

On the World Wide Web at http://www.pfeiffer.com

Printing 10 9 8 7 6 5 4 3

Editor: Arlette Ballew
Production Editor: Dawn Kilgore
Cover and Interior Page Design: Susan G. Odelson
Page Compositor: Judy Whalen
Technical Production Assistance: Shana Lathrop and Norine Spears
Illustrations: Lee Ann Hubbard

 This book is printed on acid-free, recycled stock that meets or exceeds the minimum GPO and EPA requirements for recycled paper.

Table of Contents

CHAPTER**TWO**

Understanding Change   **35**

CHAPTER**THREE**

The Dynamics of Change   **53**

CHAPTER**FOUR**

The Change Contract   **73**

CHAPTER**FIVE**

Techniques for Obtaining Commitment   **89**

CHAPTER**SIX**

Working with Resistance   **107**

CHAPTER**NINE**

Implementing Change **177**

Introduction

If you are currently in the middle of a change process, you will find the ideas in this book helpful in assisting you in your efforts. If you are contemplating a change process, you will find this approach a good way to organize the program. However, you may find this book a bit different from others on the subject of change.

WHY THIS BOOK IS DIFFERENT

There are many books and articles on the change process, and the question naturally arises, "Why, another one?" There are four answers to this question: the theory base is different, the focus is different, the intent is different, and the theme is clear.

THE THEORY BASE IS DIFFERENT

Most current approaches to change can be traced back to the early works of organization development (OD) theorists and practitioners such as Argyris, Bennis, and Beckhardt. The Gestalt approach originated in a clinical—rather than an organizational—setting. The approach to personal growth and development called Gestalt therapy is a departure from most clinical approaches, as it does not view people who have problems as "being sick" but, rather, as *choosing* a course for themselves, at some level, that is not helping them. In its simplest form, the goal of Gestalt therapy is to help people make better choices for themselves and to take full responsibility for doing so.

Fritz Perls, the creator of Gestalt therapy, pointed out that perfect therapy could be done by the therapist (or parent or change leader) asking three questions at exactly the right times (Perls, 1973). The questions are:

1. What are you aware of *right now?*

2. What do want, *right now?*

3. How are you stopping yourself from getting it, *right now?*

Gestalt therapy (or simply Gestalt) has often been described as "therapy for normals." The term "Gestalt" is a German word that refers to a clear, emerging figure. By way of illustration, it can be said that the triangle on the far right in the figure has a stronger Gestalt than the two triangles to the left of it.

Three Triangles

One might characterize the right triangle as being clearer, better-defined, stronger, less ambiguous, more complete, and in more contrast with its background than are the other two triangles. It's not good and it's not bad, it simply *is,* and the more it can be seen for what it is, the easier we can relate to it.

As it is with triangles, so it is with people. The more we can experience individuals as they *uniquely are*, rather than how we would like them to be or believe they "should be," the easier it is to relate to them and work with them.

Gestalt theory relies heavily on the use of paradox. This suggests that many things appear to be just the opposite of what they are. Some of the paradoxes that this book relies on are:

1. You change by not changing.

2. Slower is faster.

3. The more complex the change, the simpler it is to implement.

These statements may not make sense at first, so explanations are in order.

1. You Change by Not Changing. Clearly, change does result from a conscious decision to do something differently and then doing it. It also occurs by not focusing on the change but by increasing your awareness of what is happening right now. This increase in awareness allows you to see and experience the object of your attention differently and more intently. This perception *is* a change from what you previously were aware of.

2. Slower Is Faster. Most of us are familiar with the phrase, "We always have time to do it over; we never have time to do it right the first time." When we look back, there is a point in time that maximizes the implementation of each change. Much past that point, there is a tendency for energy to drain and external conditions to change and become disruptive. The result is that the final implementation may not meet the original expectations.

If you try to implement the change before the point of readiness, the usual outcome is disappointment and frustration. How often has a change been announced with great enthusiasm, only to crank down before it reached final implementation. Adrenaline runs out, we tend to become bored a little more easily, and it isn't long before we are looking for the next "quick fix."

The trick to managing change is to give it all the time it needs to ensure its positive and permanent effect—the first time. Usually, all this requires is a little more patience than we tend to expend.

One of the standard Gestalt axioms is, "Good endings make good beginnings." This means that in any effective change process, time must be given to obtain reasonable closure on each phase of the planned-change strategy prior to initiating the next step.

3. The More Complex the Change, the Simpler It Is To Implement. It is important to understand that simple structures are difficult to deal with because they have no smaller parts that can be moved. For example, a two-ton boulder is a simple structure; all it does is sit there. Two tons of gravel is more intricate in composition, but you can do more with it (e.g., make piles, make paths) and it is easier to move. For another example, suppose we are at war with another country (the boulder). We start by capturing a particular bridge (a piece of gravel).

In implementing change, one important function is to take the time to break the change down into its most basic elements. Implementing a series of small, highly controllable changes allows for greater flexibility and buy-in on the part of those who have to make the change happen.

THE FOCUS IS DIFFERENT

The approach to change management in this book varies from most others in two distinct ways. The first is that most change strategies are geared to creating change in the group setting, whereas the focus of this book is on how to work with individual concerns and issues within the group context.

When attempting to implement a specific change with an entire group, the chances are that one will view it solely as a group issue. The primary focus will be, "How will this change affect *us?*" However, it is most likely that each of the group members will experience the change and its implications as a personal issue, i.e., "How will this change affect *me?*"

Although there certainly are group issues involved in such a process, one will gain most control by maintaining awareness of individual responses and dynamics.

The second major departure this book makes is that it views change as a two-phase process. Many current change strategies acknowledge resistance as a natural response to change and offer some techniques for lessening it or overcoming it during the implementation process.

The Gestalt approach regards resistance as originating in the dynamic of "power," rather than in the "change" process and treats it respectfully as a separate, essential, and integral element of the change process.

THE INTENT IS DIFFERENT

This book is full of step-by-step, "how to" instructions for implementing change, and this is its least important contribution. What is of infinitely greater importance is that while reading this, you will have an opportunity to test the ideas presented here against your ideas about the change process. The intention of this book is not to indoctrinate you to one way of thinking so much as it is to afford you an opportunity to check—and perhaps broaden—your perspective about the change process. When you read this book, if you see some things differently, the chances are that you will be able to modify some of my suggestions to fit your style, thus maximizing their benefits.

The Contents

An overview of the chapters may provide an orientation to the message and method of the book. Each chapter deals with a specific aspect of the change process and will, in most cases, provide you with options from which to choose, depending on the situation, the nature of the change, and your own style. There are exercises in each chapter that you may adapt to meet your individual needs.

Chapter 1. Power and Self-Interest: The Driving Forces Behind Change. Power is the ability to get what you want. The change process is rooted in the ability to be clear and concise about what that is. In this chapter, power is defined, analyzed, and contrasted to several things with which it is frequently confused. The concept of enlightened self-interest is presented, and how power facilitates the change process is discussed.

Chapter 2. Understanding Change. The change continuum is presented, and eight assumptions about it are discussed. The role of the change leader is explored, and four strategic leadership options are presented. A simple and very pragmatic model for change is introduced.

Chapter 3. The Dynamics of Change. Much needless resistance to change can be avoided if the change leader knows how to structure the environment to support the change process being implemented. A process for framing the demand for change is presented as well as one for reframing it. The impacts of organizational structure and group dynamics on change implementation are discussed.

Chapter 4. The Change Contract. Starting the change process well is not a matter of luck but one of control. The use of the contract is explained as a way of setting ground rules, clarifying expectations, and developing a "partnership" in the change process.

Chapter 5. Techniques for Obtaining Commitment. Ownership in a change comes with involvement. Five group problem-solving techniques, borrowed from OD, are presented and explained. Each of these has high probability of generating group energy and high-quality results.

Chapter 6. Working with Resistance. This chapter has a purely Gestalt perspective on the subject of resistance. Resistance is a positive force in managing change and it needs to be viewed as something to be worked with, rather than as something to be broken down, avoided, or minimized. A strategy and several tactics are presented that will help you to work with specific resistances to change.

Chapter 7. Negotiating Change. The more that a change can be negotiated with those who have to implement it, the higher the probability of getting their cooperation and commitment. This chapter discusses what happens when you don't negotiate. Three negotiation styles are presented; dos and don'ts for dealing with resistors are listed; and eight important tips for negotiating effectively are offered.

Chapter 8. Situational Exclusion. Although getting everyone involved in every change may seem to be desirable, it is not always appropriate. There are times when excluding an employee from a specific change process is in the best interest of the group, the success of the change, and the employee. Two types of exclusion are discussed in this chapter. A six-step strategy is introduced for implementing caring exclusion.

Chapter 9. Implementing Change. The background considerations that support the beginning of the change process are discussed. Four six-step strategies are presented; these are to be selected, depending on whether the proposed change is externally imposed or internally generated and whether it is negotiable or nonnegotiable. For each strategy, examples are provided. A process for conducting the change meeting is also presented.

THE THEME IS CLEAR

The theme of this book is consistent with its theory base. It emphasizes a basic human value that drives the whole change process:

■ ■ ■

No human being has the right to make a unilateral decision that affects the lives of other individuals without offering them a voice in that decision.

■ ■ ■

Reference

Perls, F. (1973). *The Gestalt approach*. Palo Alto, CA: Science and Behavior Books.

Before reading Chapter 1, complete the following:

POWER ANALYZER

Directions: Before reading Chapter 1, respond to each statement by placing an "A" in the "Before" column next to the statement if you agree with it, or by placing a "D" in the "Before" column if you partially agree or disagree with the statement.

After you have read Chapter 1, complete the form again, this time responding under the "After" column. The correct answers are in the back of the book.

	Before	**After**
1. Powerful people can be identified by a specific set of attributes.	_____	_____
2. Really powerful people have the ability to intimidate and disempower other people.	_____	_____
3. The more power a person has, the less there is for his/her subordinates.	_____	_____
4. It is very important that people in an organization get along well together.	_____	_____
5. Powerful people tend not to value collaborative effort.	_____	_____
6. Powerful people value conflict.	_____	_____
7. There is a finite amount of power in any organization. Powerful people know how to get it and use it.	_____	_____
8. Powerful people are usually seen as being flexible.	_____	_____
9. Being powerful is the natural state. Nobody has to be taught how to be powerful.	_____	_____
10. Power is basically an evil force. There are better ways of getting things done in organizations.	_____	_____

CHAPTER**ONE**

Power and Self-Interest: The Driving Forces Behind Change

Change in organizations usually is a result of somebody wanting something to be different from the way it is. In a work-group setting, a change usually entails requiring people to do something differently.

We are all familiar with the law of inertia, which says that "bodies in motion tend to stay in motion, and bodies at rest tend to stay at rest." This is just as surely a law of group dynamics as it is a law of physics. For example, have you ever tried to get a bunch of lethargic kids interested in an activity and, once successful, tried to get them to stop? There are endless examples of "human inertia"; it takes an inordinate amount of energy to get a change process started—or redirected—once a decision to go ahead has been made.

The most important element in initiating any change process is the ability to formulate a clear "want." There are a lot of subtle social values that suggest that "wanting stuff" is not good. On the other hand, the clearer you are about the change you want, and the more personally determined you are to get it, the higher the probability that you will be effective. To phrase it a bit differently, your personal power and self-interest are the primary driving forces behind any change you initiate.

Thus, before you delve into the strategies and tactics of implementing a change process, you need to spend some time and effort exploring the more important question, "How are you stopping yourself from getting what you want?" More directly, "How are you disempowering yourself?"

As with most organizational buzz words, the term "empowerment" lacks a common meaning. We use the word and then hope or assume that everyone knows what we mean. We hear references to "power lunches," "power colors," and even "power ties." People talk about the need to "empower others." What is needed is a common understanding of the term "power."

DEFINITION OF POWER

A universal definition means that this is what the word means no matter where, who, or what. Power in an organizational setting is no different from power in a political or personal setting. All that is different is where it is occurring, not what it is about. Thus, a universal definition of power is as follows:

■ ■ ■

Power is the ability to get all of what you want from the environment, given what's available.

■ ■ ■

There are three elements in the definition, each of which requires an explanation.

Power Is the Ability

Most people regard power as an interpersonal phenomenon that must involve two or more people. Some attach it to a person's position, to what or whom they know, or even to what they are wearing. I contend that power is purely an ability and is *intra*personal. Just like any other ability a person has (e.g, to run, think, sing, or play soccer), the capacity for power is internal and is not subject to external influence. Of course, there may be a lot of external factors either supporting or blocking the full expression of the ability, but the ability itself is internally determined. For example, how fast you are *able* to run is a matter of internal capacity. How fast you *choose* to run frequently is influenced by external variables such as the reason for running, how it might appear to others, physical obstacles, and so forth.

Power operates in exactly the same way. There may be many external variables that influence the extent to which you choose to express your power, but the power itself cannot be affected by outside sources. Because power is purely an internal ability, you cannot empower or disempower another person, nor can anyone empower or disempower you.

This means that we can finally get rid of the popular but foolish notion that we can "empower" other people. What we can do is to remove some of the stumbling blocks that we have put up in others' paths, but the actual empowerment is up to them.

To Get All of What You Want from the Environment

A common belief is that the need for power is an internal drive that most people experience to some degree. There are myriad novels, plays, and films that focus on an individual's insatiable drive for power. The belief that people want power for its own sake is so widespread it would be silly of me to assert that it isn't so. However, to the extent that it is so, it's a darned useless pursuit. People who strive to attain power are wasting a whole lot of valuable time and effort.

In my view, the only useful function of power is to "get stuff." Wanting power for its own sake makes as much sense as wanting oats—for their own sake—when you don't own a horse. Or, put another way, having a warehouse full of batteries doesn't make sense if you don't have an appliance that runs on them.

Given What's Available

There are two reasons why you do not always get all of what you want all the time. The first is that you have somehow disempowered yourself. Some ways in which people disempower themselves are: not being clear about what they want, not taking responsibility for pursuing their objectives, putting others' needs before their own, and being overly concerned about obtaining other people's approval. I'll discuss these and other means of disempowerment later in this chapter.

The second reason for not getting what you want is that it is not available now. When this is the case, you need to recognize it, give up the pursuit of the unattainable objective, and work for something that is available.

THE NATURE OF POWER

Power has five identifying characteristics, as follows:

- It is uniquely expressed,
- It is always associated with cost and risks,
- It is neutral,
- It is existential, and
- It resides in conscious choice.

Power Is Uniquely Expressed

There is another common belief that really powerful people are identifiable by a set of characteristics. I contend that just the opposite is true. The powerful people in literature, business, and politics are usually portrayed as being steely-eyed visionaries, in their early forties to mid-fifties, who stand up straight and have great speaking voices. There probably are enough powerful people who do conform to this stereotype to keep it alive.

On the other hand, the reality in most cases is that the more a person relies on his or her own set of identifying characteristics, the more powerful he or she is going to be. For example, the executive who spends the day commanding and inspiring others and getting what he wants is clearly powerful. But when his three-year-old granddaughter scrambles up in his lap, puts her arms around his neck, and whispers, "Grandpa, please could I...?," and gets whatever she asked for, she is every bit as powerful as he is.

There is no set of characteristics that identifies the powerful person. The more you are aware of who you are and the more you value your uniqueness, the more likely it is that you will be able to effect the changes you want.

Power Is Always Associated with Costs and Risks

Every time an attempt is made to employ power, there is a direct cost and/or risk associated with it. One of the more obvious ones is that if you make an attempt and fail, your record is diminished. Another is that if you say "yes" to one opportunity, you are saying "no" to every other opportunity that might be available at the time. In addition, there are all the other costs in terms of time, effort, and consequences.

A lot of people aren't aware of the costs of being powerful when they are successful. First, really powerful people are rarely popular. They may be admired and idealized, or feared, or envied, or resented, but they rarely are genuinely liked except by those who are closest to them. Many people find it a lot easier to criticize someone else's accomplishments than to get up the energy to be successful themselves. If you have a strong need to be liked, stay away from this stuff!

Another cost is that as you continue to be successful, others' expectations of you change. You are under no particular obligation to meet those expectations; however, whether you do or you don't, it's going to cost you.

Power Is Neutral

Some people see power as something that is basically good. Throughout history, there have been "power brokers"—people who obtain relevance in their own lives by messing around in the lives of others. Yet one may ask, "How powerful are people who continually demand external validation for their own feelings of self-worth?"

There are other people who see power as something that is basically evil, something to be shunned. These people want to do something only if it can be done collaboratively. What is to be gained is of secondary importance to how it will be accomplished.

The third type of person sees power as it really is, which is neutral. In this context, power in the psychological sense is no different from power in the physical sense. *Power isn't good and it isn't bad; it simply is,* just as electricity isn't intrinsically good or bad, it just is. It is how it is used that makes a difference.

Power Is Existential

Two minutes ago is gone. Two minutes from now doesn't exist yet. The only time and place you can ever express power is in the here and now, at this moment in time. Anything that pushes you into the past, such as how things "should be," or into the future, such as worrying about what "might happen," renders you powerless for the moment.

The more you can stay aware of what is occurring right now and allow yourself to respond to the uniqueness of each situation, the higher the probability that you will be powerful—successful in getting what you want.

Power cannot be accumulated and hoarded like gold. The important thing to remember is that power cannot be stored. *Power that is not expressed is lost!*

Power Resides in Conscious Choice

One choice is simply not making a choice, and that renders you powerless.

Value statements such as "honesty is the best policy"; "respect your elders"; and "if you can't say something nice, don't say anything at all" are fine as statements of values. However, they become destructive when they are taken as unvarying rules of conduct. For example, if your boss shows you a picture of his teenaged grandchild, and you think the kid looks like nine miles of bad road, in this case, is honesty really the best policy?

Two choices are better than one, but not much better. There are three basic problems associated with most two-choice strategies. First, two-choice strategies usually try to break the either/or deadlock. They cast choices as either black or white, good or bad, right or wrong; they do not allow you to respond to the unique quality of each person and each situation.

The second problem is that frequently you can end up "on the horns of a dilemma." When the alternatives seem equal, it is easy to become stuck between them. It's much like watching a donkey starve to death between two equally distant piles of hay.

The third problem is that two-choice strategies often require you to deliver ultimatums to people. I can't think of a better way to disempower yourself than to offer me an ultimatum. If you say to me, "If you don't do this, I'm going to do...," guess who decides what you are going to do?

The magic number is three. If you are moving toward an objective and suddenly find yourself blocked, the strategy is to stop, generate a minimum of three options, and consciously choose among the three. This is a full expression of power. At the very minimum, it will keep you moving toward the objective. If it doesn't, the chances are that you are pursuing something that is not available at the time.

The same strategy applies when a request is being made of you. You have the option of saying, "Yes, I will"; "No, I won't"; or "Yes, I will, under the following circumstances." This third option allows you flexibility in getting what you want and in assisting others to do the same.

WHAT MAKES POWER WORK

There are several very simple assumptions about power that demonstrate how simple and uncomplicated the exercise of power is.

1. Power Is the Natural State. People are born powerful, i.e., with the ability to get what they want, given what's available.

2. There Is No Such Thing As Bad Human Capacity. Every human capability has some potential for both good and bad. Killing with no cause is pure evil; killing in the defense of religion, family, or country can earn you sainthood or a medal of honor. Conversely, helping people who need help is a good and caring thing. Helping people who don't need help keeps them dependent.

3. There Are No Victims. Although this can be an overstatement, it is much closer to the truth than the assumption that everybody is a victim. The fact is that if you keep doing what you've been doing, you'll keep getting what you've been getting. What you need to do is occasionally stop and ask yourself, "How is it going?" If it's not going as well as you would like, try doing something different.

4. You Are Responsible Only for Yourself. You are accountable only for what you do and the choices you make. You are not responsible for what other people do or feel. That belongs to them.

5. You Are the World's Foremost Authority on You. The more aware you are of how you are uniquely different from everyone else, and the more you *value* that uniqueness, the more you will be able to use yourself creatively, effectively, and with greater self-confidence.

6. You Are Not the Captain of Your Soul and the Master of Your Fate. Usually you have very little, if any, control over events. The law is passed, the shot is fired, the pie is thrown. What you do have total control over is how you choose to *respond* to events. In that respect, you are the captain of your soul.

HOW POWER IS LOST

As mentioned above, power is a natural condition. Everybody is born with a set of "power tools." Unfortunately, many people are taught at a very early age how to disempower themselves. Usually, this is done with the best of intentions.

The following is a list of some of the ways in which people tend to disempower themselves.

1. Saying "I Can't When You Mean "I Won't." There are a lot of things you cannot do, and that is all right. The term "I can't" means "I am powerless in this situation." On the other hand, if you state, "I can't do that," when you really can, you tell yourself as well as others that you are powerless. Try saying, "I won't," instead.

2. Letting Other's Approval of You Be More Important Than Your Own Approval of You. Of course, in certain situations, some other people's approval of you does matter, but you will never gain *everybody's* approval, nor should you want to. And no one's approval of you is more important than your own.

3. Always Putting Other People First. There are times when it may be very appropriate to put someone else's needs ahead of your own. However, if you do not recognize your obligation to take care of yourself first, you are always going to end up with the scraps, and that is your choice.

Another subtle—but no less important—aspect of this is that if you are someone else's prime source of support, by not taking care of yourself first, you are weakening that person's support system and are not as able to fill the role.

4. Asking for Permission Inappropriately. If you want to use something that clearly belongs to someone else, ask the other person for permission. However, if the ownership or accountability is in question, go ahead and use/do as you choose. If you are correct, your right to continue the action will be established. If you are wrong, you can apologize and promise not to use/do it again. It is usually a lot easier to obtain forgiveness than it is to obtain permission.

5. Not Being Clear About What You Want. You are always accountable for what you do, but you are never accountable—to anyone—for what you feel or want. Until you give yourself full permission to want what you want, and to want all of it, there is little likelihood that you'll give yourself permission to get it.

One tactic is to state what you want in the simplest, most direct way you can, with no qualifying phrases. Saying "I just wanted to say..." or "I only wanted to point out..." tells the listener that that you don't have much faith in your choice.

6. Credentializing. Credentializing is the act of responding to someone else's expertise while neglecting your own. For example, your physician has the expert credentials in the field of medicine. He can suggest any number of treatment options. However, you are the expert in what is best for you; it is your choice, not the physician's, as to what treatment you will undergo. Asking, "What do you think I should do?" is all right; it elicits an opinion. Asing, "What should I do?" is not all right; you disempower yourself that way. Remember that the other person may know more about the subject, but you know more about what is in your best interest and how to apply it.

7. Dealing in Generalities. To get better at getting what you want, you must be extremely specific about what the want is. For example: "I want to be happy" is very general; you need to state what it would take to make you happy. "I want more responsibility" needs to be defined by "for what?" and "in what situation?"

8. Demanding Guarantees. Few people fail deliberately, and some risks are just not worth taking. However, if you refuse to act without a guarantee, be prepared to stay where you are forever. Even when a guarantee is available, it doesn't promise success, it only tells you what recourse you have in the event of failure.

9. Asking a Question When You Want To Make a Statement. There is nothing wrong with asking a question when you want to gather information. However, when you want to state something, if you say "Don't you agree that...?" or "Isn't it true that...?," you lose power. This occurs three ways. First, you risk confusing the listener, who doesn't know whether you are cajoling him or her or are honestly interested in his or her response. Second, by asking the question, you risk the answer, "I would never agree with that." Third, the listener is apt to perceive the "question" as manipulation and is less apt to give you a positive or honest response.

10. Being Unwilling To Say "No." Of all the ways in which people disempower themselves, this is the most obvious. The result of this is that you could wind up working three hours overtime when you didn't want to, or you could be smack in the middle of a thirty-year marriage because you said, "I do" when you really "didn't." When you say "yes" but want to say "no," or when you withhold disagreement when disagreement is appropriate, you make yourself a victim.

Another result of an unwillingness to say "no" is what it does to the other person. If you always say "yes" when I ask you for help, regardless of your willingness, personal commitments, or ability to really help, it won't be long before I stop asking you at all. If I can't count on you to say "no" when you aren't available, I can't really trust your "yes."

POWER, SELF-INTEREST, AND THE CHANGE PROCESS

Developing an effective change process begins with recognizing that it takes power to get the change that you want. Your effectiveness as a change leader is based on your willingness to be clear and unapologetic about what you want and to have the determination to go after it.

One of the biggest errors that many change leaders make is to assume that group members will support a change for any of the following three reasons:

1. The employees knew what was expected of them when they accepted the job, so they have a social contract with the organization to support any change that management thinks is necessary.

2. The employees know what you, the change leader, want. They should provide the needed support because you are the boss.

3. The employees are expert at their jobs, and you are expert at yours. They should recognize that you know what's best for the organization.

Each of these assumptions could be correct in particular circumstances. However, in most instances they fail to consider the Law of Enlightened Self-Interest. The Law of Enlightened Self-Interest states:

■ ■ ■

In the long run, people can be counted on
to do what will be of greatest personal benefit
to themselves, individually.

■ ■ ■

This is not a measure of human frailty or a trait to be ashamed of and overcome; it is something to celebrate, for three reasons:

1. The Law of Enlightened Self-Interest is immutable. Things that cannot be changed need to be honored and worked with.

2. The Law of Enlightened Self-Interest is natural. It means that you are responsible for getting what you want.

3. The Law of Enlightened Self-Interest makes an assumption of strength. It assumes that people have the energy, foresight, and ability (power) to get what they want and need for themselves.

Enlightened self-interest does not preclude the common good, nor does it suggest that there is a conflict between what is best for the individual and what is best for the organization. What it does suggest is that there usually is a natural linkage between what is in the best interests of the group members and what is in the best interest of the organization. The change leader must be aware of this potential commonality of interests and formulate the change within this context, whenever possible.

When the change does not reflect the best interests of the group members, it is a negative test of the change itself. That is, if the change does not bode well for the people who will be affected by it, or if it cannot be stated in terms that the employees would naturally support, it should raise the question, "Do we really want or need to do this?" If the answer is "yes," then go ahead with the change but keep two things in mind:

1. Expect some natural resistance to the change effort.

2. Do not assume or imply that anything is wrong with the employees because they are responding negatively to the change.

Enlightened self-interest does not preclude putting organizational or others' needs above one's own, nor does it deny that self-sacrifice can be an appropriate response under certain conditions. What it does do is remove these responses from the status of being virtues. That is, self-sacrifice is something that we occasionally must do in order to gain an important outcome, but it is not something that we should engage in for its own sake.

There is nothing wrong with altruism. When you do something altruistic, the immediate result is that you feel good for having done it. That's the payoff.

The Power/Change Relationship

There is a direct cause-and-effect relationship between understanding and being comfortable with personal power and being an effective change leader. First, whether the demand for change is phrased as a personal want or as something that would benefit the organization, it is something that *you* want to have happen. The more you know about how to get what you want—how to express your personal power—the more likely you will be able to make a change happen.

Second, you do not have to teach people how to be powerful. Remembering that power is the natural state, all you have to keep in mind is that *power breeds power*. Simply by being powerful, you create a psychological vacuum that must be filled with a powerful response. For example, if I say to you, "What do you want to do tonight?," the chances are you'll say, "I don't know, what do you want to do?" We may never be able to decide on something. On the other hand, if I say to you, "I'm going out for coffee and dessert; do you want to join me?," you will respond with either, "Yes, I do," "No, I don't," or "Instead, how about...?"

My being clear about what I want forces you to be clear about what you want, within the same context. The process is no different in the work situation. If you say to me, "What do you think of the new safety code?," I might respond with, "I don't know, what do you think of it?" However, if you say, "I think this new safety code is far too extreme, and we need to question it!," the chances are that I will quickly be aware of my response to your statement and to the code.

Third, by being comfortable with your power, you set an example for those with whom you live and work. The more powerful you are, the more you actually "teach" power by example. If you have no problem making clear, reasonable demands of other people, you become a model for effective behavior. Because you are a leader who is doing this, you communicate to all those below you in the organization that this is an appropriate and organizationally approved way to respond.

CONCLUSION

In conclusion, it will help if you can understand power as it really is: a part of your daily existence. It is as important and as natural as laughter, caring, competence, or any other capacity you have that contributes to living well. By becoming more comfortable with and confident in you personal use of power, you not only increase your own effectiveness, you also facilitate the empowerment of those with whom you live and work.

On the following pages, you will find several activities that allow you to take the concepts discussed in this chapter and begin to apply them to your unique situation and ways of doing things. There will be hands-on activities and questionnaires at the ends of the other chapters, as well. Although there is no demand that you complete all of the activities and questionnaires, it is a good idea to tackle a few, at least, before you continue to the following chapter. They will afford you an opportunity to become comfortable with the concepts and will help you to personalize the information in this book.

CHANGE-LEADER ACTIVITY: DEFINING THE THEME

Concept/Objectives

A theme is to a book what a mission is to an organization or a set of values to an individual. The theme gives the book its unifying purpose. Because I feel so strongly about the theme of this book does not mean that you have to in order to have this book be of value to you. What it does imply is that it would be helpful for you to be clear about where we differ so that you can modify the information in this book to support your set of values.

Directions: Read the theme statement below and then answer the following questions pertaining to it.

THEME STATEMENT:

No human being has the right to make a unilateral decision that affects the lives of other individuals without offering them a voice in that decision.

1. I support the theme of this book.

1	2	3	4	5	6	7
Not at all						Very

2. The theme makes sense to me because:

3. The theme does not make sense because:

4. As I see things, the theme would be better stated as follows:

CHANGE-LEADER ACTIVITY:
YOUR VIEW OF THE CHANGE PROCESS
Concept/Objectives

Whether a proposed change is one that you initiated or one that was initiated elsewhere and you have to implement it, how you view the change process will have a lot to do with how much of your energy goes into aiding or resisting the change. Becoming clear about and more comfortable with how you view change will give you a lot more control over the process.

Part 1

Directions: Respond to the three questions below as honestly as you can. Their significance will be explained at the conclusion of this activity.

To what extent:

1. Am I interested in the change process?

1	2	3	4	5	6	7
Not at all						Very

2. Am I confident in my ability to handle the change process?

1	2	3	4	5	6	7
Not at all						Very

3. Am I looking forward to reading the rest of this book?

1	2	3	4	5	6	7
Not at all						Very

Part 2

Directions: As you begin to think about the change process, think about how you can adapt this information to your personal style and unique situation. You can begin this process by working with the three basic questions that were mentioned in the introduction.

Question 1: What am I aware of, right now?

As of this moment, what are the forces that are driving change in your organization? List as many as you can think of, e.g., organizational policy, environmental conditions, boss's whim, and so forth. Be as specific as you can. _Don't restrict or censor your responses._

1. _____
2. _____
3. _____
4. _____
5. _____
6. _____
7. _____
8. _____

Now, list all the forces that are blocking change in your organization right now, e.g., unions, traditional viewpoints, limited resources, and so forth. Again, be as specific as you can and try not to censor yourself.

1. _____
2. _____
3. _____
4. _____
5. _____
6. _____
7. _____
8. _____

In looking at both lists, make a judgment about the extent to which your organization is currently resisting or supporting change.

Totally Resists						Totally Supports
1	2	3	4	5	6	7

Question 2: What do I want, right now?

Now that you have been thinking about your organization, what would you like to see happen right now? Do not try to justify your wants or be concerned about their practicality or availability. The more specific and complete you can be, the better.

What I'd like for the organization:

1. _____

2. _____

3. _____

4. _____

5. _____

6. _____

7. _____

What I'd like for my unit and the people in in:

1. _____

2. _____

3. _____

4. _____

5. _____

6. _____

7. _____

What I'd like for me:
(This is the most important category. Include things off the job as well as those that are job related.)

1. _____

2. _____

3. _____

4. _____

5. _____

6. _____

7. _____

8. _____

9. _____

Question 3: How am I stopping myself from getting these things right now?

(Remember, although there are many organizational blocks to change, as you noted in question 1, you still stop yourself from getting what you want more than any other single source. For example, how did you stop yourself from listing all nine wants for yourself in the above section?)

1. _____

2. _____

3. _____

4. _____

5. _____

6. _____

7. _____

8. _____

9. _____

Finally, having gone through this activity, please respond to the questions below:

To what extent:

1. Am I interested in the change process?

1	2	3	4	5	6	7
Not at all						Very

2. Am I confident in my ability to handle the change process?

1	2	3	4	5	6	7
Not at all						Very

3. Am I looking forward to reading the rest of this book?

1	2	3	4	5	6	7
Not at all						Very

If the answer to any of these questions is higher than the response you gave to it earlier, you are already operating under the assumptions on which this book is based.

CHANGE-LEADER/GROUP ACTIVITY: DISEMPOWERING SURVEY

Concept/Objectives

One of the guiding axioms of the Gestalt approach is that, although there are some very real constraints in the environment that are blocking you from getting what you want, you stop yourself more than all those constraints put together do!

This activity is designed to help you gain more control over the ways in which you are disempowering yourself. Although this might turn out to be a somewhat uncomfortable process, the payoff is that you will take more control over your own life as a result.

Part 1

Directions: Think back to a change situation—preferably work-related—that resulted in a noticeable failure or disappointment for you. This event should be one that still has some "sting" to it.

1. What was the event? Briefly describe it with a beginning, middle, and end.

2. What were (are) you feeling?

3. What were the effects on the organization of this event having occurred?

4. What were the effects on you personally?

Part 2

With some very few exceptions, solid success or failure experiences in organizations are rarely the result of only one person's input or action. The key to gaining control is to be able to accurately assign the specific responsibilities to those to whom each responsibility belongs. (Note that the operative term is "responsibilities," not "blame.")

OTHERS:

Specifically, who contributed to the event and what did each do, or fail to do, that led up to the event?

Person	Contribution
1. _____	_____
2. _____	_____
3. _____	_____

SELF:

The truth is that there are very few real victims in today's organizations. We somehow contribute to the results with which we end up living. This section is designed to assist you in taking back full responsibility for *your* part of the event. In doing this, as uncomfortable as it might seem, you simultaneously reown the power that you unknowingly gave away.

CHECKLIST

Directions: To identify some ways in which you stopped yourself from getting what you wanted out of the event, respond quickly with a "yes" or "no" to the following options.

Did I:

1. Assume I was powerless, without checking it out?   Y   N

2. Care more about someone else's approval than I did about getting what I wanted?   Y   N

3. Put everybody's needs ahead of my own?   Y   N

4. Ask for permission, inappropriately?   Y   N

5. Take the time to be clear about what I wanted?   Y   N

6. Get bogged down in someone else's credentials?   Y   N

7. Neglect stating what I wanted in specific, behavioral terms?   Y   N

8. Demand a guarantee?   Y   N

9. Scare myself into immobility?   Y   N

10. Attempt to justify my want to others and/or myself?   Y   N

SCORING KEY

1-3 Yes Answers: Could be appropriate in this situation. What you wanted simply may not have been available at that time.

3-5 Yes Answers: Indicates that you clearly collaborated in not getting what you wanted in this particular situation.

6 or more Yes Answers: Indicates that you were taking little or no responsibility for getting what you wanted.

In looking at your responses, what would you do differently today to increase your probability of being successful, were you able to go back and do it over?

GROUP ACTIVITY: DIAGNOSING THE GROUP
Concept/Objectives

In introducing change to most groups, you can count on a variety of reactions. Getting a feel for how your group is reacting to a change can save you considerable time, effort, and stress.

One of the biggest mistakes any change leader can make is to assume that a group will respond to a change in the same way that it responded to a previous one. Each change is a new occurrence. It will have some similarities with and many differences from the changes that preceded it. The more you can focus the group's energy on the uniqueness of the change, the higher the probability that you will be able to implement it effectively.

Distributing the following form to your group and reviewing the results before the first implementation meeting will set you on the right path.

Note: The accumulated data from this form can be shared with the group as a way of initiating the change process.

CHANGE DIAGNOSIS FORM

Directions: Answer the questions below as honestly as you can. Your unbiased opinion is greatly needed, regardless of what that opinion is. Please _do not_ sign this form or in any way identify yourself unless you choose to do so.

Proposed Change:

1. I think this change is beneficial to the organization.

1	2	3	4	5	6	7
Strongly Disagree						Strongly Agree

2. I think this change is beneficial to me.

1	2	3	4	5	6	7
Strongly Disagree						Strongly Agree

3. I intend to support this change.

1	2	3	4	5	6	7
Strongly Disagree						**Strongly Agree**

4. I think the group, as a whole, will support this change.

1	2	3	4	5	6	7
Strongly Disagree						**Strongly Agree**

5. What I like most about the proposed change is...

6. What I resist most about the proposed change is...

7. One thing that would make this change better or more acceptable is...

8. Something else that needs to be considered is...

GROUP ACTIVITY: REOWNING GROUP POWER

Concept/Objectives

The power of a group is synergistic, i.e., it is greater than the sum of the combined contributions of members. The same can be said for power loss; it, too, can be greater than the sum of the combined energies. Nevertheless, power is still always a matter of individual control. How a group becomes more or less effective in getting what it wants—or resisting what it doesn't want—is usually a matter of loss of individual contribution. That is, group members have colluded with one another to blur their individual differences and soften their areas of disagreement and conflict. This activity is designed to help a group reestablish clearer and stronger contacts among its members.

Directions:

1. Have the group members take the following Group-Power Analysis Survey individually and anonymously.

2. Summarize the data and present the summary to the group, being careful to present it as group data.

3. Lead a group discussion of the survey outcomes.

4. Reestablish group norms by consensus.

GROUP-POWER ANALYSIS

Directions: This survey is designed to assess how well your group is working. Please answer each question to the best of your ability. Do not identify yourself.

1. Open disagreement in the group is becoming less frequent.

1	2	3	4	5	6	7
Strongly Disagree						Strongly Agree

2. There seems to be as much, or more, emphasis on getting along well as there is on accomplishing group objectives.

1	2	3	4	5	6	7
Strongly Disagree						Strongly Agree

3. Anger, even when expressed nonthreateningly, is frowned on.

1	2	3	4	5	6	7
Strongly Disagree						Strongly Agree

4. All decisions are reached by consensus, whether everybody's input is needed or not.

1	2	3	4	5	6	7
Strongly Disagree						Strongly Agree

5. Strongly disagreeing with or challenging group consensus is becoming less and less popular with the group.

1	2	3	4	5	6	7
Strongly Disagree						Strongly Agree

6. The group members have a hard time agreeing to disagree.

1	2	3	4	5	6	7
Strongly Disagree						Strongly Agree

7. When disagreement does surface, people tend to state it as softly as possible.

1	2	3	4	5	6	7
Strongly Disagree						Strongly Agree

8. Open conflict seems to frighten the group.

1	2	3	4	5	6	7
Strongly Disagree						Strongly Agree

9. The group tries to do everything as a team.

1	2	3	4	5	6	7
Strongly Disagree						Strongly Agree

10. I can count on positive feedback from the group members a lot more than I can count on their negative feedback.

1	2	3	4	5	6	7
Strongly Disagree						Strongly Agree

SCORING KEY

7-14: Your group values individual differences as much as it does cohesive team work. Proceed with the change effort.

15-28: The group is still capable of maximizing individual contribution and perspective; however, differences are starting to blur. Go ahead with the change, but stay alert, particularly if one or two questions produced particularly high scores.

29-42: The group is becoming more concerned with process issues than it is with task issues. The change initiative could easily end up taking a back seat to the need for everyone to get along well together. Don't proceed until you have addressed a few of the more challenging questions.

43-60: Your group is overly process oriented and probably does not have the capacity or the perspective to effectively address the change at this time. Start looking for ways to break the "we-ness" that is debilitating the group.

60+: Your group is, in all probability, in the throes of "groupthink." Bring in some third-party help to assist the group in realigning itself under more realistic norms.

CHAPTER**TWO**

Understanding Change

THE CHANGE CONTINUUM

Most people perceive change as unpleasant, disruptive, and something to be avoided. The paradox is that the only constant is that change will occur. In fact, we adapt to change all the time and do it very well.

In thinking about change, we need to recognize that change isn't good and it isn't bad, it just *is*. Change itself is neutral.

One way to envision change is as a continuum. All human characteristics and capacities operate in polarities, e.g., good/bad, strong/weak, tall/short, and so forth. The capacity for change also can be viewed as a polarity. The range can be "no change" (e.g., life in a Trappist monastery) to "constant change" (e.g., a recruit's first two weeks in basic training).

In the illustration that follows, the left segment describes the condition of no change. This position is the traditional view. It is focused on the past; archly conservative in its values; and regards almost any change as a threat to the established order, values, and norms. The belief is that if it's new, it's bad. Key policy makers and people of influence who hold this position tend to be in their mid-fifties and early sixties. At dinner, these people compare what they are eating with the best meal they ever had.

Although this position provides stability, comfort, and minimum threat, it also carries the seeds of boredom, lack of opportunity, zero growth, and increasing levels of individual and interpersonal stagnation.

NO CHANGE

Traditional
Past
Change is Bad
Values What Was
Older
Blindly Resists Change
Stagnation

PRODUCTIVE CHANGE

Now
Change is Inevitable
Values What Is
Wide Age Range
Honors Resistance
Growth &
Effectiveness

CONSTANT CHANGE

Dynamic
Future
Change is Good
Values What Might Be
Younger
Suppresses Resistance
Chaos

The Change Continuum

The right segment describes the condition of constant change. This position is the dynamic view. It is focused on the future. The belief is that if it's new, it's good. Any change is seen as positive, and any resistance to change is viewed as being behind the times and counter to group norms. Key decision makers and people of influence in this range tend to be in their late twenties to mid-thirties. At dinner, such people think about what they will have for breakfast.

Although this position provides energy, excitement, and activity, it also produces motion without meaning, mindless jargon, the tendency toward superficial treatments, and an increasing inability to focus on what is really important. The move is toward chaos. In their rush to leave the traditional behind, many of today's organizations have rushed into this range of organizational norms and values and are not much better off for having done it.

In the center of the continuum is the condition of productive change, which can be described as the pragmatic view. This position is focused on what is happening now and is characterized by flexibility. Change is seen as inevitable; how one responds to it is a matter of conscious choice, even when that choice—situationally—is for the status quo. Policy makers and people of influence in this range are of all ages within an organization. At dinner, such people tend to concentrate on enjoying the meal.

A paradox within the range of productive change is that "one changes by not changing." That is, when you focus on what is happening right now, the increased awareness resulting from that focus *is* change.

To illustrate this, stop reading for a moment and look at some object in the room. Notice its color, unique shape, dimensions, texture, even its temperature. Is there something about it that you have never noticed before? Does your interest in it increase or decrease? Either way, if the answer to the last question is "yes," change has occurred.

How one chooses to respond to a new condition is a matter of conscious choice. The decision is best made by comparing what is wanted with what is available and then considering the current conditions that are supporting and/or blocking the change.

In the productive range, the move is toward growth and effectiveness. It is this position that results in the smoothest transition from one state to the next.

TWO ASPECTS OF THE CHANGE PROCESS

Initiating change is a two-phase process. Phase 1 is presenting the change, and phase 2 is working with the resistance that seems to accompany every change. Most people do a pretty good job in phase 1, planning and then presenting the change, and then they stop, not realizing that there are aspects of the change that people don't like and that the job is only half done. Even when a change goes smoothly and people seem willing to accept and implement the change, there usually are some parts of the change that they find uncomfortable or threatening.

It is very likely that different people will have different concerns about the change. This does not imply that you should attempt to work through every piece of resistance that the change may engender. This would be tedious and self-destructive in many cases. What it does suggest is that you need to be aware that some resistance is almost always present, and you need to make a conscious decision whether to address it or not. Strategies for working with resistance are presented in Chapter 6.

In the change continuum, each range has its own unique response to resistance, just as it has to change. The position of "no change" tends to resist change reflexively because it sees change as being bad. The position of "constant change" tends to suppress resistance because it sees change as being inherently good. The position of "productive change" honors resistance because it sees resistance as an inherent part of the change process.

Eight Assumptions of Productive Change

There are eight assumptions on which the productive change process rests.

1. Change is best facilitated by developing ownership in the change process.

2. Change will occur most easily in an atmosphere of enlightened self-interest.

3. People do not resist change; they resist pain or the threat of it.

4. People actually tend to resist the opposite of change, which is boredom.

5. Power is the ability to get what you want; resistance is the ability to avoid what you don't want. Resistance is a subset of power, not of change.

6. Resistance is best dealt with by honoring it rather than suppressing, avoiding, or minimizing it.

7. People can work best with others' resistance by first understanding and accepting their own resistance.

8. Change leadership involves helping people to make better choices in light of the current realities and then assisting them in taking full responsibility for pursuing these choices.

The Time-Change Continuum

The flow of change is as natural and unavoidable as the flow of time. In fact, the two are closely related. Because time is dynamic and ongoing, so—to some extent—are all the things that occur within it.

As a matter of illustration, in the time it took you to read the paragraph above, you became aware of its content. That's a change. Had you chosen to do something else, that would have been a change, too. Had you chosen to do nothing, you would have experienced an additional period of rest—a small but real change. At the very least, the tide would be a few minutes higher, the earth a few minutes older, and you a few minutes closer to your next crisis, meal, or nap.

The main difference between time and change is that the flow of time is unavoidable *and* uncontrollable, whereas the process of change is unavoidable but, in many cases, quite controllable if we choose to control it.

TWELVE STEPS IN THE CHANGE PROCESS

The change process,[1] in its most basic form, comprises twelve steps, as illustrated by the following.

The model is an illustration of one of the paradoxes raised earlier: the more complex the change, the easier it is to implement. Almost any change, from the simplest (e.g., buying a new jacket) to the most complex (e.g., "rightsizing" a large organization) involves this twelve-step process. A brief illustration may be helpful.

1. Environmental Event. As mentioned above, time flows and so do the events that occur within it. A frost kills a coffee crop in Brazil; a patent is awarded for a new microchip; and I accidentally rip the sleeve of my favorite leather jacket.

---

1 This model is adapted from "The Syntax of the Contact Episode," in *Gestalt Therapy Integrated: Contours of Theory & Practice,* by Erving and Miriam Polster. Vintage Books, New York, 1974. Used with permission.

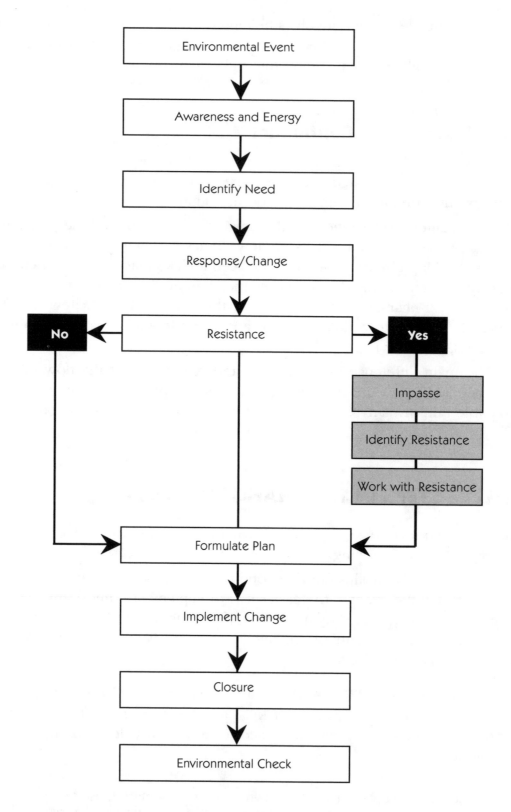

The Change Process (Polster & Polster, 1974)

THE CHANGE LEADER

2. Awareness and Energy. Of all the events that are occurring around me, the one that I become aware of is the torn jacket. This is the environmental event that has the most relevance to my life right now. As my awareness of the event increases, energy is marshalled in response to the awareness. I might be heard to swear. At this point the environmental event is said, in Gestalt terminology, to have "figure." This means that the particular awareness is standing out from my awareness of all other events that are occurring, all of which can be described as "ground," as they have faded into the background. My attention and frustration are focused solely on my torn jacket.

3. Identify Need. The awareness is that my jacket is torn; the energy is available to take it to the next step, which is to determine what my need is in this situation. I can ignore it, repair it, or replace it. If it were an inexpensive, old, ugly jacket that I wore only occasionally, I might consider myself lucky to be rid of it. In that case, I would not have a need, and the next environmental event would become figural.

4. Response/Change. Looking at my options, my response in this instance is the decision to replace the jacket. This is the change.

5. Resistance. As soon as I identify the change I intend, resistance to that change may arise. More is said about this phenomenon in Chapter 6. Suffice to say that resistance needs to be seen as a positive and integral part of the change process.

■ ■ ■

The change is in service to getting you what you want.
The resistance is in service to protecting
you while you are getting it.

■ ■ ■

Not every change is accompanied by resistance. For instance. there may be little or no resistance to the following changes: the organization decides to provide long-term disability insurance at no charge to employees; the company gives everyone a personal parking space; my wife offers to buy me a great leather jacket for my upcoming birthday. On the rare occasion when a change produces no resistance, we proceed immediately to step 7 in the change process.

6. Impasse. Most often, a change generates some resistance, and an impasse results. An impasse occurs when the option has an equal capacity to attract and repel; the resistance to the change is nearly equal to the energy driving the change. In "psychobabble," this is called an approach/avoidance conflict.

7. Identify Resistance. The resistance to the change usually comes out in a series of "yeahbuts." "Yeahbut" means "no." For example:

- "I want to buy a new leather jacket."
- "Yeahbut, I can't afford it."
- "Yeahbut, the new styles are ugly."
- "Yeahbut, it'll take forever to break it in right."
- "Yeahbut, I'll have to go shopping."

The clearer the change, the clearer the resistance that rises to meet it. Clear resistance makes the change process a lot easier to work with.

8. Work with Resistance. The strategy now is choosing a resistance and working with it, not attempting to ignore it or override it. First, you need to increase your awareness of the resistance and appreciate its impact. Once the resistance is honored, it has the effect of modifying the change to more realistically accommodate the current conditions. For example, in response to my resistance, I could say to myself, "I don't want to spend more than $150.00" or "Maybe I can do this through catalogue shopping."

9. Formulate Plan. Once the resistance has been worked with, a plan for implementation must be formulated. For example, I will visit shops that are close to home, feature clothes that I find tasteful, and offer a selection that falls within my price range.

Without a plan, I am likely to have a miserable time and not accomplish what I have set out to do. I could easily end up looking at jackets out of my price range or style and buy something I don't really want, simply out of impatience and frustration.

10. Implement Change. The plan is now put into action: I go to the stores that I chose to look for the jacket. There are two concerns in this stage. First, I need to periodically check the plan to make sure that it is working for me. Sometimes conditions will change and make the plan less practical or workable. For instance, if it is just before Christmas, prices may be higher than I had anticipated. Maybe I need to wait until the sales after the holidays.

In discussing the impasse in step 6, I mentioned the approach/avoidance conflict created by the balance between the move to make the change and the resistance to it. The second type of conflict that can emerge is an approach/approach conflict. For example, I find a jacket that I really like at the right price. Instead of buying it, I continue to search, always hoping to find something just a bit better. Finally, I find another jacket that I like just as much as the first one. Once again, I get stuck. I am equally attracted to both choices, and I render myself immobile. It's much like the donkey who starved to death between two piles of hay. There is no way to resolve such a dilemma easily, but the clearer you are about what you want, the *less* likely it is to happen. The more indecisive you are, the *more* likely it is to happen.

11. Closure. One Gestalt axiom is that "Good endings make good beginnings." Once a change has been successfully implemented, an essential and often neglected step is to obtain closure. Closure implies that the need has been fully met and acknowledged. This takes time and conscious effort but is well worth it!

If I take a little time to assure myself that I made the right choice and that I enjoy it, I can be finished with the issue of buying a jacket and can get on with the next environmental event in my life. I will probably do things like look at myself in mirrors when I am wearing the jacket, appreciate positive comments about the jacket, or look for more opportunities to wear it.

12. Environmental Check. This step, like step 1, environmental event, is passive rather than active in nature. Nevertheless, it is an important step in the change process because it identifies when closure has been achieved.

The important aspect of step 1 was that something in the environment became figural. The importance of step 12 is that it signifies when the change issue completes its journey from *figure* to *ground*. The current issue has been completely resolved, and all of your or the organization's energy can now be focused on the next figural issue.

I chose the example of replacing a jacket for two reasons. First, it is a true case. Secondly, it is a neutral example that most people can easily relate to regardless of their organizational identities or concerns. I hope that the example will highlight the ease and natural flow of the change process. Almost any change that you can identify, from the simplest to the most complex, will follow roughly the same twelve-step process.

The process is described in order to give you an appreciation for how simply a process can work. It is not intended to be a step-by-step recipe that should be followed rigidly. Many of the steps will occur quickly and quietly, in a different order, and will be initiated by different people, depending on the unique nature of the change and the environment in which it occurs. The trick is to understand the basic nature of the change process and have faith in your ability to respond appropriately.

THE ROLE OF THE CHANGE LEADER

The change leader is the person who wants the change to happen and is in a position to work with the group to make it happen. The role of the change leader is to provide a process that will facilitate a specific change easily and effectively with minimum disruption and with maximum support from the group members.

The change leader usually is the manager or supervisor of the group that has to deal with the change, but this is not a requirement. A group member can initiate and implement a change (such as an idea for changing a specific work procedure), as can a quality improvement team, a human resource representative, or someone else.

It is important to realize that there is no one best style of change leadership. Many "experts" state that the only way to facilitate change effectively is to use a participative or democratic leadership style. Although this style is probably the most effective in a majority of cases, it is by no means the only appropriate style for effectively managing change.

THE FOUR BASIC STYLES OF CHANGE LEADERSHIP

Change leadership can be defined as the ability to obtain willing compliance to change. The more that you can facilitate a person's willingness to accept and implement change without resenting it—or resenting you for having required it—the more you are an effective leader in that situation.

As we all know, situations are constantly changing, people are constantly changing, and conditions are constantly changing. What it takes to manage change is the ability to stay flexible so that you can respond to what is going on. The more you can introduce the change in terms of what is presently happening, rather than in what "should be" happening or what might happen next, the easier time you are going to have working with your people in facilitating the change.

Change-leadership style is somewhat different from the leadership styles used in managing work. Every change leader has a unique style. Each style is made up of some combination of the four prototype styles: autocratic, participative, supportive, and laissez faire. Everyone manages change best in his or her own way, but backup styles should be learned for versatility in different circumstances.

Autocratic

In the autocratic style, the change leader makes the demand, and the group is expected to respond. It is best used when:

- the demand is simple and there is little or no interest on the part of the group, or
- the demand is externally imposed and nonnegotiable.

Application

Autocracy is an effective approach to managing change when the change is not particularly important to anyone. An example is determining what the new color will be in all the restrooms in the building. Autocracy saves time; when used appropriately, it may reduce resistance to a change because people are not having their time wasted.

Autocracy is also the appropriate style for managing change when the change is externally imposed and there is no opportunity for negotiating anything. An example is instituting a policy of no facial hair because of possible interference with safety masks. Implying that there is some choice in a change that is mandated will increase employees' frustration. It is better to state what the change will be and then let the employees openly and safely state their dissatisfaction with it and get it out of their systems.

Participative

In the participative style, the change leader is involved with the change and negotiates the change with the group. It is best used when:

- the group's input is needed to maximize the change outcome,
- heavy resistance is anticipated, and/or
- maximum ownership in the change is wanted.

Application

The participative change-leadership style is the one most frequently used because it maximizes both individual input and ownership in the final implementation. This style is characterized by the change leader and the group working together to make the change happen. It is the style to consider first if there are any negotiable elements in the change and there is a high need for input from the group members. An example is an employee-involvement team formed to recommend a way to reduce accidents in the loading area.

The participative approach is also very effective when there is a large amount of resistance to the demand for change. A change leader who is knowledgeable about working with resistance can maintain control of the group process and facilitate the group members' finding ways to work with the elements that are blocking their acceptance of the change.

Supportive

When using the supportive style, the change leader assists the group in developing a process so it can deal with the change.

The supportive style is appropriate when the group is competent to create and implement a change but needs the change leader's support in conducting a meeting. This may be the case when working relationships and trust among the group members are low. An example is when a work group is relatively new, and the members do not know one another well enough to have developed good communication patterns or high trust. The change leader focuses on the group's process in working on the change and makes sure that everyone has a chance to speak, that conflict is handled reasonably, and that the atmosphere is a relatively safe one. The change leader does not get involved in making the change happen.

A second use of the supportive style is when the group requires outside assistance or support to make the change happen and the change leader knows how to get it. An example would be when a department is converting to a new software application, and access to company training resources is needed.

Laissez Faire

In the laissez faire (hands-off) style, the change leader describes the change or the need for change, answers questions, sets boundaries, and then leaves the group on its own. It is best used when the group is highly competent to respond and there is little or no resistance to the change. An example is when an effective research and development team is asked to respond quickly to a customer's change in job specifications. In such a case, the change leader may have little task expertise in comparison with the group members. This approach to managing change is most effective when the group members have the interpersonal skills to work well together.

Reference

Polster, E., & Polster, M. (Eds.). (1974). The syntax of the contact episode. In *Gestalt Therapy Integrated: Contours of Theory & Practice*. New York: Vintage Books.

CHANGE-LEADER ACTIVITY: CHANGE-LEADER ANALYZER

Instructions: For each of the eight situations that follow, indicate which of the four basic change-leadership styles would be most appropriate. The correct answers are in the back of the book.

Situation 1.

A new piece of equipment has been bought by the purchasing department and is scheduled to be installed in your work area in two weeks. The employees are happy with the existing equipment. Productivity has been averaging 120 percent of standard for the last six months.

The change-leadership style you would choose in this situation is:

Autocratic ____   Participative ____   Supportive ____   Laissez faire ____

Situation 2.

A new OSHA regulation mandates that a particular type of wraparound safety glasses be worn in all fuel-processing areas. Previously, the workers had the option of choosing their own glasses, so long as they met regulations. Some of the workers have even personalized their glasses.

The change-leadership style you would choose in this situation is:

Autocratic ____   Participative ____   Supportive ____   Laissez faire ____

Situation 3.

A quality-action team has been formed to develop a supervisory- performance survey. Once the team has developed the survey and received approval, it will distribute the survey to the entire work force at your location.

The change-leadership style you would choose in this situation is:

Autocratic ____   Participative ____   Supportive ____   Laissez faire ____

Situation 4.

Beginning the first of next month, all employees will be required to park in the north parking lot rather than the east parking lot.

The change-leadership style you would choose in this situation is:

Autocratic ____   Participative ____   Supportive ____   Laissez faire ____

Situation 5.

Customer complaints have risen your department by 12 percent over the last three months. The department needs to find a better way to respond.

The change-leadership style you would choose in this situation is:

Autocratic ____   Participative ____   Supportive ____   Laissez faire ____

Situation 6.

A group of top consultants have been hired to analyze the company's marketing strategy and recommend a new one. The company policy is to have the external team headed by an internal manager.

The change-leadership style you would choose in this situation is:

Autocratic ____   Participative ____   Supportive ____   Laissez faire ____

Situation 7.

The organization has adopted a set of values that will drive business and human resource decisions in the future. Each division has been told to create a code that describes how it will incorporate each of the stated values into its daily operations.

The change-leadership style you would choose in this situation is:

Autocratic ____   Participative ____   Supportive ____   Laissez faire ____

Situation 8.

A cross-functional work unit has just been formed. It is made up of specialists from different parts of the organization. The unit's task is to redesign work procedures in the division.

The change-leadership style you would choose in this situation is:

Autocratic ____   Participative ____   Supportive ____   Laissez faire ____

CHANGE-LEADER ACTIVITY:
CHANGE-LEADERSHIP STYLE INVENTORY
Concept/Objectives

Leadership is an art, not a science. Leadership style is as personally distinctive as any other set of characteristics that identify a particular individual. The more you can identify and increase your comfort with your own unique approach to leadership, the more easily and confidently you will be able to guide your group through the change process.

One way to view change-leadership style is that each individual style is made up of some combination of three pure *influence* styles: supportive, aggressive, and logical.

Directions: Each item in this inventory contains an incomplete sentence followed by three different endings. You are to distribute ten points among the three endings to show to what extent each ending is characteristic of you. Always use all ten points, although you may give an ending zero points.

Respond as honestly as you can. Because the purpose of this inventory is to help you to identify your change-leadership style, there are no right or wrong answers.

> _Example:_ I would characteristically describe myself as:
> A. _3_ Easy going   B. _6_ Tough   C. _1_ Logical

1. As a change leader, my tendency is to:

    A. ___ Be supportive B. ___ Show the way C. ___ Explain

2. I feel most satisfied when I can:

    A. ___ Help others B. ___ Take the lead C. ___ Solve problems

3. People who know me see me as:

    A. ___ Understanding B. ___ Ambitious C. ___ Practical

4. When a direct report resists, I tend to:

    A. ___ Respond with empathy B. ___ Demand compliance C. ___ Explain my position

5. I view resistant direct reports:

    A. ___ With dread B. ___ As a challenge C. ___ As a necessary evil

6. When a direct report expresses dissatisfaction with the change with which we are working, I tend to:

    A. ___ Give in B. ___ Minimize the problem C. ___ Explain my approach

7. At my worst, I am apt to:

   A. ___ Withdraw B. ___ Become hostile C. ___ Be overly concerned with details

8. My strong points as a change leader lie in my being:

   A. ___ Empathic B. ___ Directive C. ___ Analytical

9. People who know me best see me as being:

   A. ___ Trusting B. ___ Strong C. ___ Practical

10. When dealing with an organizational change, I tend to rely most on:

    A. ___ My direct reports B. ___ My own experience C. ___ Data input

11. My most comfortable role as a change leader is as a:

    A. ___ Helper B. ___ Guide C. ___ Planner

12. When a direct report is unsure about a change, I usually use the opportunity to:

    A. ___ Help him/her get clearer about his/her wants

    B. ___ Persuade him/her to my view C. ___Provide more data

13. When a direct report resists my advice regarding a change, I am apt to feel:

    A. ___ Insecure B. ___ Hostile C. ___ Misunderstood

14. When conflict erupts during the change process, my tendency is to:

    A. ___ Soften it B. ___ Encourage its expression C. ___ Get to the cause

15. In the change-leadership situation, I find it easier to be successful when I can be:

    A. ___ Friendly and outgoing B. ___ Alert to opportunities C. ___ Methodical

SCORING KEY

_____ **A answers** — Supportive influence style
_____ **B answers** — Aggressive influence style
_____ **C answers** — Logical influence style

Interpretation: The higher the score for each pure style, the more influence that element has on _your_ basic leadership style. Remember, there is no preferred style. The objective of this inventory is to help clarify your present style and put you more at ease with that style as it is, not as it "should be."

If you are presently comfortable and effective as a leader, this inventory will provide you with some idea about how you are going about it. If you feel that you could be doing a little better, look to the lowest rated style for some direction as to where you might best put your initial efforts.

CHAPTER**THREE**

The Dynamics of Change

FRAMING THE DEMAND

Any change that is being initiated requires—demands—a different response on the part of organizational members. How difficult the process will be, how successful the effort will be, and how effectively the resistance will be handled are determined in large part by how clear and concise the initial demand is.

Tuning in to WII-FM (What's in It for Me?)

There are three ways in which you can present, or "frame," the demand for change. You can appeal to people's selfishness, selflessness, or selfness.

Selflessness: "I get by, by disadvantaging myself." This means always putting other people first, always being the last to state what you want, always being the first to give up. The important term is "always." Most people have an altruistic side and will do something simply because it helps someone else or because it is of benefit to the organization. This is to be appreciated and may occasionally be called on to support a change. However, it is not a good position on which to base most demands for conformance or change.

Selfishness: "I get what I want at the detriment of others." An example is a promotion opportunity in which there is room for only one person to move up. Thus, selfishness may be appropriate if the situation does not allow more than one person to succeed.

Selfness: "I get what I want and I exploit nobody." A good example is the "Jack Spratt" nursery rhyme, in which everybody gets what he or she wants for dinner. Almost everyone is interested in doing something that is good for the organization or work group; however, people are most interested in doing what is of the greatest benefit to themselves, particularly if it benefits the organization as well. Selfness is a good basis for framing demands for change as well as for developing positive, long-term organizational relationships.

There is a finite amount of altruistic energy available to each individual. Every time someone does something for someone else out of a sense of simply wanting to help, a little of that energy is used up, and there comes a time when there isn't any left. It then takes a while to rebuild the supply. When an individual has run out of altruistic energy and there is a new demand that he or she do something for the benefit of the organization, conformance to the demand will produce *resentment*. This condition is to be avoided at all costs, because it results in the destruction of working relationships and sabotage of the change process.

A variation on appealing to selflessness—and one that is just as dysfunctional—is an appeal to company loyalty. Again, this might be appropriate in a particular situation; however, it is not effective as an overall strategy for introducing change.

Loyalty is not a personal characteristic; it is a response to environmental conditions. It is a measure of the *organization's* worth. When an organization promotes personal growth, personal dignity and respect, and quality performance, loyalty to that organization is an appropriate response. It can be called on to support a certain amount of unpopular change. If an organization exploits its members or treats them disrespectfully, allows inferior materials or processes, or the like, being loyal makes no sense.

In general, presenting a demand in terms of what is good for the organization and assuming that people continually will be willing to sacrifice their own best interests for the sake of the organization is naive, at best. The most this approach can offer is everyone "singing the company song" and giving half-hearted and minimal compliance.

On the other hand, there are several reasons for basing a demand for change on selfness. First, it is the easiest and most reliable way to obtain commitment. The more the change legitimately can be framed in terms of personal benefits (e.g., opportunity for promotion), challenge (e.g., an increase in responsibility), or fun (e.g., more freedom on the job), the more receptive the employees will be.

By framing the change in selfness, you also send a very powerful message: that people are important as individuals and that what they need is respected. This is a good way to begin to strengthen the individual sense of self-worth.

Finally, and most important in terms of outcomes, the selfness approach generates a more natural and unguarded response. That is, rather than being confused about what they "should be feeling" or how they "should be responding," people feel free to tell you what they are feeling and how they are responding. In such an environment, people can support the change process more easily. By broadcasting over WII-FM every chance you get, at the very least you will keep them tuned in.

Characteristics of a Well-Framed Demand

A well-framed demand has the following five characteristics. It is:

- outcome oriented,
- stated in behavioral terms,
- specific rather than general,
- consistent with the organization's values and mission, and
- clearly understood.

The following example illustrates the five characteristics.

"The policy of reserved parking spaces for specific people will be eliminated as of the first of next month."

1. Outcome Oriented. A demand should describe the condition that the change will bring about (results), rather than describe the process (action) of changing. Thus, the above example is preferable to: "People should stop using preferred parking as of next month."

2. Stated in Behavioral Terms. Demands should focus on what is to be done rather than on how people should feel or think about the change. The best way to complicate the change process and increase resistance is to attempt to try to alter people's attitudes about the change rather than their behavior. Again, compare the above example to: "We expect employees to cooperate with the new policy of no preferred parking, beginning the first of next month."

3. Specific Rather than General. The more the demand is stated in specific terms, the easier it will be to implement the change. What the change is, who it affects, when and where it will take place, and (if appropriate) why the change is occurring all are essential in making the change easier to implement. Compare the example above to: "Certain special perks will be eliminated."

4. Consistent with the Organization's Values and Mission. The change must be seen as reflecting the true values of the organization. For example, suppose that one of a corporation's stated values is "equal dignity of all members, regardless of level." It would seem hypocritical to maintain a reserved parking policy for senior executives in the face of this value.

5. Clearly Understood. A well-framed demand meets the famous KISS criterion: "Keep it simple, stupid." The fewer the words, the simpler the words, and the clearer the demand, the better.

If the values or the conditions that have precipitated the change are clearly understood, or if the change is self-evident, the demand need not include the reason for the change. However, if the reason for the change is not clear, a statement such as, "Due to our value of equal dignity, the policy of reserved parking spaces..." would be helpful in providing the necessary background. Nothing will confuse a demand for change or increase needless resistance to one more than to have people think that the change is arbitrary or someone's whim.

Presenting the Demand

A well-framed demand contains clear components and clarity about negotiability.

The Components of the Change

Probably the best way to present a change is to include the five dimensions of who, what, where, when, and why. We are not going to discuss "how" until much later in the process. The purpose is to present the change as completely and succinctly as possible. "Who" means who will be involved or affected by the change and who will not. "What" includes the specific details of the change. "Where" refers to site areas that may be included or excluded from the change. "When" is when the change is expected to begin. "Why" is the reason that the change is being implemented.

An example of presenting a demand is as follows.

"Because of a recent change in Federal regulations, safety glasses will be worn by everyone entering Buildings C, D, and F, effective immediately."

Clarity About Negotiability

It is very important at the beginning of the change process to clarify what is negotiable and what is nonnegotiable about the intended change. The change leader needs to be really clear about this.

Some changes will be totally nonnegotiable, like the example concerning safety regulations. Some may be negotiable, but just aren't worth people's time and effort to get involved (for example, changing the cafeteria's catering service). Most changes have some parts that are negotiable and some that are not.

It is vital that you tell your group members which elements of the change are negotiable and which are not. The worst thing you can do is to indicate that it might be possible to modify the change, get people involved in the modification process, and then find out that what they are working on is carved in stone.

Confusion about the negotiability of the demand decreases your credibility. It also will increase the participants' resistance to the change. If the group knows from the outset what is not negotiable, the reasonable expectation is that everything else is open to discussion.

REFRAMING THE DEMAND

The process of reframing does not mean to frame again. It means to frame differently. As I have said, most change generates some resistance. Although there are effective ways of dealing with resistance, the best thing to do is to avoid it whenever possible. Reframing is one good way of doing this.

In discussing the change continuum in Chapter 2, I said that all human characteristics operate in polarities, e.g., good-bad, strong-weak, rigid-flexible, and so forth. Events operate in the same way: every human experience has potential for a positive or a negative outcome; every challenge has potential for success or failure; every party has potential to be entertaining or boring; every relationship has a possibility of ending up in friendship or enmity; and every change has a possibility of being accepted or rejected.

If we lose sight of the polarity, we may develop tunnel vision. Particularly when a change is perceived as unpopular, we may fail to see the positive effects that might be inherent in it. Although it is important to recognize the potentially negative aspects of the change that are bothering us, it is equally important to recognize what this specific change might be doing for us. Once we are aware of both sides of the issue, we are better able to make clear choices about how to respond to the change.

Incidentally, how good or bad the outcome of change is is determined, in large part, by the environmental conditions that support the change process. Some of these are as follows:

- what the desired change is,
- how the change affects people, and
- the costs involved in implementing the change.

The event of making the change, itself, is neutral.

Reframing is the process of expanding the demand so that both potential outcomes are obvious. It is particularly helpful when the change being demanded is initially perceived as being on the negative side of the polarity. In its simplest form, reframing means adding the phrase, "but that means..." to the demand. For example:

"Starting next month, employees will pay 15 percent of their medical insurance costs, but that means there will be no layoffs."

or

"The new policy is that all sales reps will have their sales reports in by the end of each week, but that means that sales reps will have accurate computerized reports by the following Wednesday."

You can use reframing effectively when the initial resistance to the demand is high and people are responding from a basically emotional position. If you are going to use reframing early in the process, make sure that you honor the negative aspects of the change, as stated by the employees. You need to listen to their objections fully and completely before you attempt reframing. If you meet employees' resistance with an attempt to show them the positive side, you will probably lose your credibility. The function of reframing is not to get people to like the change but to have them see that along with the negative aspects there are a few positive ones.

Reframing also can be used as a regular part of any change process to help the employees see the whole picture and the potential of the change more clearly.

THE BEST-WORST OPTION

If the proposed change is highly controversial, and the group interaction may be emotionally charged, you can add the best-worst option as a step just after you present the change for the first time. The best-worst option is identifying the polarities mentioned earlier. The difference is that you are using it as a controlled group process, rather than as an individual technique.

Ask everyone to write down the worst possible outcome that could result from the proposed change. (Always work in the predicted direction first.) Then ask the group members to write down the best possible outcome that could occur if the change went into effect. Allow them no more than five minutes to do this. Go around the room and collect the statements from each individual, then list the outcomes in two separate columns on a flip chart.

There is no need to discuss the statements. Merely having both the positive and the negative expectations stated, visible, and roughly equal in number will provide the balanced perspective needed to approach the change from a rational position.

TEN SUGGESTIONS FOR WORKING WITH GROUPS

A lot of factors affect the change process, beyond the specific change being demanded and the resistance that may arise. The following are some hints about working with small groups that can open up various options and help the change leader to work better with the group members in implementing the change.

1. Parkinson's First Law: Work Expands To Fill the Time Available.

This law of group dynamics suggests that a group will use the time it has to complete a task. If a group has thirty minutes in which to complete a task, it will tend to use thirty minutes; if it has an hour to complete the task, it will tend to take the hour. Obviously, the law does not apply to extremes, such as giving the group either five minutes or two hours to complete a thirty-minute task.

Allowing enough time *minimally* is best—enough time for the employees to get actively involved in the process. It is better to allow a little less time than is needed than it is to allow too much time.

2. Work Groups Tend to Function Best with Six Members and Usually Should Not Exceed Nine Members.

There is a geometric increase of word flow with each additional member in a group. Six is the ideal number to maximize the diversity of input and opportunity and the time to interact. As the group increases from six members, the word flow increases, and individual styles begin to exert greater influence. The time available for each member to speak is reduced, the more aggressive or outgoing group members tend to dominate discussions, and the more quiet members tend to withdraw. If a group has more than ten members, you should consider dividing the group into two groups of five.

3. Group Members Should Work on the Change Interactively As Much As Possible.

The more the change leader can have the group members interact, the higher the probability that a solution will emerge that all can buy into. The basic approach is to have the group members talk about the change, make suggestions, and modify it as much as possible, so long as there is something negotiable in the change or its implementation.

You should have something interactive planned for members to do in regard to working with the change. For example, you could have them develop a reframing list or have them break into small groups to discuss the pros and cons of the change. If you provide group members with a constructive process to work with, they will convince themselves much more easily than you could convince them.

4. Seating Should Be Arranged in a Circle.

It is important that all group members be approximately equidistant from one another and can see one another, and that there is no dominant position in the seating arrangement. Where people are physically located in a group has a lot to do with how dominant they are in relation to other group members. This is a subtle but important dynamic. If the group must work at an oblong, conference-type table, the change leader can maintain equality by taking a chair on the long side of the table, rather than at an end.

5. Synergy Is to a Group What Energy Is to an Individual.

The word "synergy" refers to the total energy of a group. The synergy of a group is greater than, and different from, the sum of the combined energies of the group members. An example of synergy is the observation that an automobile is greater than, and different from, all the parts from which it is built.

With synergy, a group has the potential of producing a solution that is more effective and more satisfactory to each member than the best of what each individual might have generated.

6. Syntality Is to a Group What Personality Is to an Individual.

Syntality is the behavioral characteristics of a group, parallel to the personality of an individual. This aspect of group dynamics is important to the change leader, particularly if there is any chance of variation in the group membership as the change is being introduced.

When a new person is added to the group, it becomes a different group. You only have to look at what happens to the interpersonal dynamics of a family when a new member joins. New alliances are formed, new resentments may appear, and different needs begin to surface. It is important to keep this in mind as you work with your group to implement or deal with change.

7. *The Medium Is the Message.*

When planning to announce and work with a change, be sure that you allot enough time for the process and that the group can work in a comfortable environment that is free of interruptions. These elements are necessary to get the job done, but they also convey the message that "this is important and worth the time we are taking."

It is *not* a good idea to introduce a change by saying to the group in passing, "Oh, by the way, beginning on Monday the work day starts a half-hour earlier."

Frequently a change is presented as a simple demand without the change leader being aware that there might be heavy resistance lying in wait to sabotage the effort. A demand that could be resented and resisted when stated one way might be perceived as a workable issue when stated a different way. This is particularly so when the change affects individual choices or preferences. For example, simply stating that beards and mustaches will no longer be permitted is asking for open warfare. If the demand is presented as a safety concern relating to the fit of gas masks for working with toxic materials, at least the change makes sense.

By stating the purpose of the change and what its proposed benefits are, you create the probability that some of the resistance will be offset. This is particularly true if there is some opportunity for the employees to explore other options. Examples include forming a committee to look into other makes of gas masks or exploring a standard that would permit some types of beards and mustaches that would fit under the masks.

8. *There Is a Direct Relationship Between the Amount of Involvement in the Change Process and the Commitment to the Outcome.*

The theme of this book is "No human being has the right to make a unilateral decision that affects the lives of other individuals without offering them a voice in that decision." This underscores the assumption that one of the most potent forces that characterizes us as a species is the need for control over our own lives. Whether it is a toddler insisting that she be allowed to feed herself or a worker being given the option of flex time, all things being equal, people will commit more to outcomes that they have participated in creating.

When planning a change, be clear about what is negotiable and what is not, with a view toward encouraging the group members to become involved in the process. The more their suggestions are considered and incorporated into the final outcome, the higher their commitment will be to that outcome.

As a brief example, when I taught at a university, I told my students, "I need an objective measure of your performance for grades." I'd then divide them into small groups and have them determine the grading procedure they thought would be best. With little exception, I would adopt their suggestions and I never had to deal with the assertion, "This grade isn't fair."

9. The "Gadfly Option"

Group process and opinion can form very quickly. They are influenced by many things other than the proposed change. Not the least of these is how the group sees itself, particularly in terms of being "cooperative" or "stubborn." The "gadfly option" is one way to counter unstated group norms that restrict open opinion and input.

If the change is basically unpopular, the gadfly option consists of designating one person in the group to look *only* for what is right about the change. For example, a group member says, "Gee, we now have to pay 15 percent of our own insurance premiums." The gadfly replies, "Right, but keep in mind that this is the lowest rate being demanded in the industry."

The gadfly option is just as important if the change appears to be popular. It is just as important to know where the hidden traps may be in a positive change as it is to be aware of the potential benefits in an unpopular change. It's like the old saying, "If it sounds too good to be true, it probably is."

For example, a group member says, "Great, we can move to flex time." The gadfly replies, "Sounds good to me; however, we have to consider how that will affect the production schedule."

10. Don't Hold the Chalk.

One of the biggest myths of group dynamics is that the person who is "holding the chalk"—writing on the flip chart or taking notes—is in charge.

This probably comes from the fact that this person is standing in front of the group. Actually, this person is the *least* influential because he or she is simply doing what everyone else is telling him or her to do.

As the change leader, you should not dominate the group, but you should not be subservient either. When working with the change, have a volunteer take the notes, which allows you to either lead the group or sit back and pass the reins to another group member.

COMMUNICATING THE CHANGE

There are three basic ways to communicate a change. They are as follows.

The Whole Group

If the change involves the whole group, announce it to the whole group. This is time effective and appropriate. It helps to stop rumors and partial facts from leaking out to the group members. If one or two members are affected by the change in a particular way, the details can be reviewed with those individuals after the general announcement.

The Individual

If the change involves only one group member, discuss the change privately with that person. If it is a negative change, such as a layoff, a private meeting will save the member from embarrassment and/or having to deal with the pity of coworkers. If it is a positive change, such as a promotion, it will give the individual an opportunity to assimilate it and to plan how others should be informed.

Informal Leaders

If the change is going to produce some heavy resistance, knowing the informal leaders in the group and discussing the change with them first is helpful. In the first place, they can tell you how they think the change will be received. Also, they will be useful in providing suggestions about how to proceed. If they can support the change, they may be willing to help with its implementation. Finally, by consulting them ahead of time, you are acknowledging their status as informal leaders, which will help to obtain their support and to establish a long-term working relationship with them.

Timing

A change can be introduced too quickly and result in chaos, or it can be announced and not acted on for months, resulting in the buildup of anxiety. The best strategy is to announce the change as close to the time for active planning and implementation as possible.

Most people will agree that living with ambiguity is, at best, disquieting and, at worst, intolerable. There seems to be almost universal consensus that the worst possible news is preferable to—and easier to live with than—the condition of not knowing. If details of a change are not clear, most people tend to make up bad news to fill in the temporary void in information.

Despite this tendency, in the long run you are better off to simply state that you don't know the details and force people to live with ambiguity, rather than attempt to confirm a rumor, have to deny it later, then modify your statements in light of new information. The best you can do is to state, "Like you, I don't know what the status of that is. I am going to have to wait along with you to find out what is happening."

CHANGE-LEADER ACTIVITY: CENTERING THE CHANGE

Concept/Objectives

Change is an ongoing process, whether we like it or not. We can stay in control of a change process by staying focused on what is happening as it unfolds. Many change processes are badly mismanaged because the change leader is focused either on the past or on the future.

Focusing on the past can establish false expectations, because the current conditions are always different from those of the past. Thus, dealing with a proposed change in terms of how it should be tends to blur one's awareness of what is going on right now. You can't attend to what was and what is simultaneously.

Being future oriented is no more effective than looking to the past. When the focus is on the future, the tendency is to rely on hope. Although hope is preferable to despair, it tends to imply that there is nothing else that can influence the change. It is important not to relinquish your ability to do anything about the change.

Being _centered_ or _grounded_ is the Gestalt terminology for being firmly anchored in the present. It implies that you are fully aware and in touch with what is happening in the environment and what your reactions are to these events. The more centered you are, the more control you have over the change process and everything else.

Directions:

1. State the proposed change:

2. List all the ways in which the members of your group _should_ react to the proposed change, given your experience in working with them.

3. List all the ways you _hope_ your group will react to the proposed change.

4. Now, how do you think they _will_ react?

CHANGE-LEADER ACTIVITY: FRAMING EXERCISE
Concept/Objectives

The Gestalt theory base emphasizes the importance of taking full responsibility for your own values, actions, and wants. This principle is as important in the change process as it is in any other aspect of one's job or private life.

How well a demand for change is considered by others is frequently a measure of how effectively it is presented to them. The three basic contexts for framing a demand for change are:

- *Selflessness:* "Only be concerned about others";
- *Selfishness:* "Only be concerned about yourself"; and
- *Selfness:* "Pursue your own objectives and avoid harming anyone in the process."

<u>Directions:</u> For practice, cast the following demands for change in each of the three contexts.

<u>Example:</u> **Flex time**

Selfless: In order to meet the company's needs for on-time delivery, a policy of flex time will be instituted. Please check with your supervisor to see how you can choose a work schedule that will be of greatest value to the company.

Selfish: A policy of flex-time is being instituted, effective the first of next month. Scheduling requests will be granted on a first come-first served basis.

Selfness: A policy of flex-time is being instituted, effective the first of next month. Please discuss your schedule with your supervisor so that your working hours are of the greatest advantage to you and to your unit's production schedule.

Change: Mandatory overtime

Selfless:

Selfish:

Selfness:

Change: Safety glasses are to be worn at all times

Selfless:

Selfish:

Selfness:

Change: No smoking

Selfless:

Selfish:

Selfness:

Now repeat the exercise using two real or possible changes from your work environment.

Change:

Selfless:

Selfish:

Selfness:

Change:

Selfless:

Selfish:

Selfness:

CHANGE-LEADER ACTIVITY: TUNING IN TO WII-FM
Concept/Objectives

Any change has a better chance of earning active support when it can be described in terms of the person's best interests. Saying how a proposed change will be of personal benefit to an employee is more effective than linking the change to company loyalty, altruism, or guilt.

Directions:

1. List each person in your group and state what the most important driving force is for each one.

Example:

Name: *Dave*   Drive: *Task accomplishment*

Name: *Sally*   Drive: *Autonomy*

Name: _____   Drive: _____

Name: _____   Drive: _____

Name: _____   Drive: _____

Name: _____   Drive: _____

Name: _____   Drive: _____

Name: _____   Drive: _____

Name: _____   Drive: _____

2. How could you present the proposed change in a way that would appeal to each group member's primary drive?

> Proposed Change: **Flex time**
>
> Name: *Dave*   Appeal: *Opportunity to work more directly with the West Coast sales reps.*
>
> Name: *Sally*   Appeal: *More control over her time.*

Name: _____ Appeal: _____

Name: _____ Appeal: _____

Name: _____ Appeal: _____

Name: _____ Appeal: _____

Name: _____ Appeal: _____

Name: _____ Appeal: _____

Name: _____ Appeal: _____

CHANGE-LEADER ACTIVITY: REFRAMING EXERCISE

Directions: After reading each of the following statements, reframe the change to indicate some potential benefit (from the perspective of the people who have to implement the change). Have some fun with this!

1. Because of current customer demands, the work day will start and end thirty minutes earlier, but that means...

2. The company cafeteria will be closed for the next three weeks to allow for the installation of new equipment, but that means...

3. Because of the consolidation plan being implemented next week, each person with less than five years' seniority will be asked to share his or her office space with one additional person, but that means...

4. As of the first of next month, the organization will be changing from mainframe to personal computers for all personnel, but that means...

Now try to reframe a few situations from your work or home life that appear to be unpleasant. Again, have some fun with this.

CHAPTER**FOUR**

The Change Contract

Most people, to some degree, like surprises in the nonaccountable parts of their lives. Birthday parties are nice, unexpected gifts are fun, and good news from any source is almost always welcome.

Surprises are usually appropriate off the job but, almost without exception, are *inappropriate on the job*. This is because the surprised person has no idea what is coming. This violates the theme of this book, because a surprise is a unilateral decision made by one person that affects others without their agreement.

The sooner people are made aware that change is on its way and what their role is going to be in that change, the less unnecessary resistance you are going to have to contend with. This brings up the issue of the contract.

I I I

A contract is an agreement between the change leader and the group members, freely negotiated and entered into, that defines and clarifies expectations for how people will deal with one another as part of the change process. The purpose of the contract is to provide a means of starting and proceeding together. The contract should be negotiated as the very first step of the change process.

I I I

The contract covers two broad areas. The first is defining the roles and responsibilities of the change leader and the participants. The second is defining the process through which the change will occur. This usually refers to guidelines for how the change meetings will be conducted.

The contract is the best means you have for assuring that there won't be any surprises in dealing with the change. It creates a safe environment in which differences of opinion can be discussed and it maximizes the probability that commitment to the change will occur to the extent that it is available.

ELEMENTS OF THE CHANGE CONTRACT

Although there are no strict rules about what should or should not be included in a change contract, the following are some suggestions about what you might want to include. Keep in mind that the purpose of the contract is to provide the safest and most creative environment for openly addressing the change.

There are six essential elements to be negotiated in any change contract. These address:

- The change leader's role and responsibilities;
- The roles and responsibilities of the group members;
- Definitions of acceptable and nonacceptable behaviors during the change process;
- A determination of how disagreements, resistance, and confusion will be handled;
- Nonwork and environmental issues; and
- The process for changing the contract.

The Change Leader's Role and Responsibilities

In looking at the discussion of the nature of change leadership in Chapter 2, it is clear that there are many options available to you in terms of how you define your role. Some of the things that you might want to consider are:

- the style you are most comfortable with,
- the group's expectations of you,
- the time in which the change has to be implemented,
- the importance and impact of the particular change, and
- how much group involvement is needed.

How you lead the change *must be negotiated* with the group members and will reflect how involved with the change you wish to be. For example: Is your role to facilitate or to interact? Will you always vote or will you vote only to break a tie? How about your right to veto any suggestion because, as leader, you will be personally accountable for the implementation of the change? What is your role if the group cannot reach consensus?

Being clear about your view of your role and presenting that as the first part of the contract to be negotiated sets the stage and makes a clear statement about how you see the leadership function. If the first thing you do is negotiate, rather than simply declare your leadership role, the group more easily understands its own power.

The Roles and Responsibilities of the Group Members

If you are working with a new group or an ad hoc committee, establishing clarity about members' roles early in the process has three distinct advantages. First, it will highlight your role as change leader and allow you to state what is important to you in terms of creating productive group norms. Second, it helps to establish a value of openness and proactiveness because the contract is being negotiated rather than imposed. Third, negotiating rules of conduct as the first order of business creates a safe environment, because it is quite possible that not everyone will know or like everyone else in the group.

If you are leading a change with your own work group, the definition of roles and responsibilities is even more important. Just as the group's expectations for you might shift as a function of the change process, your expectations might change for them, as well. As you have defined and negotiated your role with them, you can also define and negotiate *their* roles with them.

Take the time to plan ahead, to think about what specific behaviors and responsibilities you would like the group to assume. Keep in mind that the goal is to assure the best implementation of the change with the greatest commitment on the part of the members. By way of illustration, some of the new or different roles and responsibilities you might want to consider are as follows:

▮ If you disagree with something, it is your responsibility to state your disagreement openly and clearly.

▮ If you are going to be late, you are obligated to let someone know as soon as possible.

- If you cannot attend a meeting for some reason, you are obligated to send a substitute if at all possible.

- You agree not to discuss this change outside of this group until it has arrived at consensus.

- If you think the group is getting bogged down in trivia or going off the track, you have an obligation to say so.

One additional advantage to developing this process with your own group is that it provides you with an excellent opportunity to have the group experiment with new and different behaviors that might be more productive or supportive in the day-to-day work environment. These processes, e.g., consensus decision making and group problem solving, can be introduced much more easily in a temporary and nonthreatening environment.

Acceptable and Unacceptable Behaviors During the Change Process

Whether the change is large or small, whether it involves an established work group or an ad hoc committee, each person participating in the change process will come into it with different expectations about how things should be. As the change leader, you should deal with these elements before you start addressing the change itself. First, it will preclude a lot of unnecessary interpersonal conflict over trivia, once you begin to address the change. Second, it will give the participants an opportunity to become acquainted with one another's working styles before they begin working together on the change itself.

If the change is a small one or one that can be dealt with in a single meeting, this element may not be as important as some of the others. On the other hand, if there is to be more than one meeting, being clear about what is acceptable and unacceptable can help to avoid unnecessary frustration.

This element deals with things like not being late, smoking, room temperature, and side conversations. Eliminating such issues at the beginning eliminates potential hassles during the process.

How Disagreements, Resistance, and Confusion Will Be Handled

The relevance of this element will vary with the nature of the change being discussed. There might be some argument in discussing a minor change in work procedures, but a change in policy concerning vacations could be extremely volatile.

Whether it is expressed or not, you can count on some resistance to every change. You want to set the stage for that resistance being expressed as soon as it arises. You are always better off having the resistance stated early and openly than you are having it festering and unexpressed, in the pretense that it isn't there.

Some parts of this element that need to be stated are: all questions and concerns are welcome; it's okay and safe not to like this change and to say so; disagreement is appropriate so long as it is focused on the change. Take some time to determine what guidelines are comfortable for you and then frame this element.

Nonwork and Environmental Issues

This element deals with taking care of the small, but sometimes very distracting, things that can interrupt a change process. If the change meetings are to be short and conducted as part of the regular work day, this element will not be very relevant. However, if the meetings are to be long and/or conducted offsite, it probably will be. It helps to be clear at the outset about such things as starting and ending times, meal breaks and available food service, other breaks, how phone calls and messages will be handled, parking, suitable clothing, smoking, and so forth. As with all things, the more the group members can influence such matters, the less resistance you will encounter during the process.

The Process of Changing the Contract

The last element in the contract needs to relate to the contract itself. Although it is called a contract for lack of a better term, there is nothing binding about it. The purpose of the contract is to provide a means of starting together and proceeding slowly and surely. You need to point out that the contract can be modified at any time during the change process. It must be done openly and with all members participating to the extent that they are interested in the proposed modification. Until the time that someone suggests a change in the contract, the things agreed on are the rules of operation.

These six elements of the contract are core issues, in that almost all change processes will require that some attention be paid to each of them. They are not necessarily the only elements of the contract. Other concerns may need to be addressed, depending on the nature of the change. For instance: how new people will be brought into the group; how responsibility will be assigned and/or negotiated; and who should or should not be included in the actual change process. Chapter 8 contains a more in-depth discussion of this last issue.

THE BENEFITS OF THE CONTRACT

If it is negotiated before work on the change begins, the contract provides the change leader with positive control over certain aspects of the change process. Once the change process has begun, it is extremely difficult to change the rules or to redefine what is expected from group members without severely increasing resistance to the change.

The Contract Surfaces Relevant Information About the Change

One benefit of using groups to create and implement change is that no two people will see the same thing exactly the same way. The contract creates a safe environment for negotiating differences of opinion about the change. If the participants know ahead of time which behaviors are appropriate and which are not, open expression of ideas and feelings is more likely to occur. Anything that encourages a free flow of information and ideas increases the probability that the most appropriate process for implementing the change will emerge.

The Contract Reduces Needless Resistance

A lot of the resistance encountered in dealing with change is focused on the experience of change itself and the anticipated problems that the change might bring about.

One source of needless resistance that can be avoided arises if confusion is allowed to exist after the change process has started. Ambiguity about the full nature of the change; how the change might affect various individuals or groups; what is expected in terms of group interaction; and other similar issues create a confused environment that becomes psychologically risky, if not downright dangerous.

By taking the time to address these, and similar concerns, as the first step in initiating change, change leaders can avoid a lot of the unnecessary resistance and self-defense that arise from people not knowing what to expect and not having a hand in the events in which they are involved.

It is not enough to clear up the confusion before the change process starts. There must be clarity about how new confusion and conflict will be handled once the change process begins. The contract provides a process for ensuring an effective response to these concerns.

The Contract Promotes Interaction and Involvement

One of the biggest advantages to a contract is that it gives the change leader and the group the opportunity to talk about pertinent issues before they have to deal with them. The contracting process is helpful in several other ways. First, the interaction is occurring in the change environment, which allows people to understand how others regard the change without having to defend anything. Second, the contracting process allows you to redefine your role with the group, if you choose to, before the actual change process starts. Third, it allows the group to begin to buy into the change process before it has to work on implementing or accepting the change itself.

The Contract Establishes Ownership of the Change and Shared Leadership of the Process

Although there is no question that your role as change leader is established in the contract, you can share as much of the leadership with the group as you like, through use of the contract. The more leadership you can share, and the more you can allow the group members to have control over getting what they want, the easier it will be to effect the change.

SUBCONTRACTING

Sometimes a change process has a very high chance of being volatile. This could be for any number of reasons. For example, the change could be very controversial, the change could result in some people being harmed (e.g., a severe reduction in budget or other resources), or the group could have a history of poor interpersonal relationships. Regardless of the cause, if you anticipate that the change process could explode into an interpersonal free-for-all or implode into a solid mass of silent, passive resistance, you might want to expand element 4—how disagreements, confusion, and resistance will be handled—into a separate subcontract.

How Disagreements, Confusion, and Resistance Will Be Handled

One of the distinctions of Gestalt theory is that it values conflict and attempts to *manage* it, rather than to merely resolve it. Conflict is seen as a source of energy, and anything that provides energy to a group process is, by definition, good. The challenge is how to manage that energy productively.

This can be done by negotiating a separate contract to respond to conflict issues before any formal work on the change has occurred. The subcontract can be created as a separate issue after the main contract is negotiated or it can be incorporated in the main contract, depending on how much importance you want to place on it.

In presenting the subcontract, make it as simple and nonthreatening as possible. One of the risks in discussing the potential for conflict is that you may create a self-fulfilling prophecy. That is, by overemphasizing the potential for conflict, you make people a little more uptight and guarded, so that they are more prone to a defensive response.

A few possible elements of a subcontract follow.

One Issue at a Time

Often in the course of a conflict, a separate and unrelated issue will emerge. Agree to bracket this and deal with it later. Sometimes the issue that surfaces turns out to be the real problem, rather than the symptom that was being discussed. It doesn't matter which issue is tabled and which one is addressed at the time, so long as a choice is made and everyone agrees with it.

Speak Only for Yourself

There seems to be a tendency for people to use "we" and "our" when they are really speaking for themselves. Agree that individuals are to take responsibility for their own opinions by starting statements with "I think..." or "My opinion is...."

Everyone Has a Right to His or Her Opinions

Establishing the legitimacy of individual differences makes it much safer to for people to state their views and disagreements openly. It is very important to establish that no one is at risk for disagreeing. When people can disagree openly and easily they will find it that much easier to agree openly and easily.

Avoid Reacting to Unintentional Remarks

Sometimes in the heat of the moment, people say things they don't really mean. It is a good idea to establish a norm that if someone says something in the heat of the moment but doesn't really mean it, it's okay to let it go.

Each Person Is Responsible for Not Stating Disagreement

Most people are aware of all the bad things that might happen if they state disagreement openly. They may not realize the bad things that can happen if they don't. This guideline states that people are free not to disagree openly with what's happening, but if they don't make their views known, they give up the right to criticize it later on.

Keep Focused on the Change

Change meetings are not intended as arenas for dealing with past interpersonal problems of group members. You may let such problems emerge if you think it will improve the group's process. However, the focus should be on the impact on the group and the process, and no one should be allowed to attack an individual. You can keep the environment safe by having the group members agree ahead of time that only disagreements related to the intended change will be considered appropriate for these meetings.

Similarly, organizational dissatisfaction that is irrelevant to managing the intended change can arise. You can suggest that the group members agree that issues dealing with company policy, personnel matters, or past injustices will not be discussed in this forum.

It's All Right To Question Someone

Differences in perceptions abound. Stress that just because someone does not believe what someone else says does not mean that he or she thinks the first person is a liar. It means that the second person has a different view or a different source of information. It is helpful to establish a norm that makes it all right for members to ask questions to clarify information, so long as the focus remains on the topic, not on "showing up" the individual.

Make Requests Specific

One purpose of the subcontract is to provide a means for making positive changes in the process. There can be a norm that anybody can make any request, as long as it is specific, behavioral, and time bound. For example, rather than stating "I want more support," a member can be coached to state, "I'd like someone to help me with the statistics on the Digby project next week."

NEGOTIATING THE CONTRACT

The main purpose of the contract is to increase the probability of group members' ownership of the change process and the change. How the contract is implemented must be consistent with what you are trying to accomplish. The contract must be negotiated with the group rather than imposed on it.

Probably the most effective way of negotiating is to have the proposed contract written down before starting the meeting. Be sure that everyone knows well ahead of time what the purpose of the meeting is.

Start the meeting by stating that all are here to discuss the new change and that it's important to take a little time to set some guidelines for how people would like things to proceed. Point out that although this is called a contract, it is negotiable at any time during the meeting, so long as the change leader and the group members do it together. Stress that you have prepared a contract but that there are no "musts." Then go over the contract a point at a time, stopping after each one to be sure that it is clear and that group members agree to it. Continue until you have worked through the entire contract.

If you are going to use a subcontract for managing conflict, state that the proposed change is somewhat controversial and that feelings seem to be running high. Point out that some people may be guarded about stating their feelings and views openly and that an open environment is essential for dealing with the change. Say that, to make this a safe place for people to express themselves fully, you would like to suggest a few ground rules for conducting the meeting. Then proceed to work on the subcontract the same way you did the main contract.

The amount of time that will be required to develop and refine the contract is a function of the group's syntality, its size, and the potential impact of the proposed change.

CHANGE-LEADER ACTIVITY: CREATING A CONTRACT

Directions: Use the questions that follow to create a contract for implementing a change that is upcoming or one that you would like to see. Try to select something from the job environment; if that is not relevant at the moment, pick a change that you would like to see in your private life.

1. What is your role in this (e.g., leader, facilitator, gadfly)?

2. What new roles and/or responsibilities do you want the group members to assume?

3. Are there certain behaviors that you want to have happen?

4. Which specific behaviors are inappropriate?

5. What concerns do you have about conflict?

6. Do you intend to use a subcontract? If so, what elements will you include?

7. What nonwork and environmental issues do you need to negotiate with the group (e.g., starting and ending times, length of work day, offsite concerns)?

8. What other concerns do you need to be aware of?

CHANGE-LEADER ACTIVITY: THE UPWARD CONTRACT
Concept/Objectives

Just as a contract provides a safe and open environment in which your direct reports can work with the change, you might need the same thing when accepting a demand for change from your boss or someone else in higher authority.

Directions: On the form below, identify the elements that would provide you with the optimal work context for dealing with the change with your boss or someone else in higher authority. When you have completed this, think about negotiating this with your boss.

Change:

What problems do I anticipate in negotiating this change with my group?

How much time will I need to complete the negotiation effectively?

What physical, financial, or other organizational resources will I need?

Physical:

Financial:

Other:

What specific support do I need from my boss to implement the change with my employees?

What would I like my boss to do?

What would I like my boss <u>not</u> to do (at least not without checking with me first).

What kind of access do I want my boss and me to have with each other during this change process?

What decisions would I like reserved for myself?

What decisions are clearly reserved for my boss?

What concerns do I still have that I need clarity on from my boss?

CHAPTER**FIVE**

Techniques for Obtaining Commitment

You can implement a change by forcing compliance, you can purchase people's compliance, and you can wheedle others into compliance. Many techniques work if all you want is compliance.

For simple changes that do not require much energy or commitment from people, compliance often is enough. It is best to use the simplest method that will obtain the desired outcome. The problem is that many, if not most, of the changes demanded of people in today's organizations require a lot more than passive submission to the demand for change.

Getting true commitment to a change effort is a critical part of the change process. It relates to the central theme of this book that was stated earlier: No human being has the right to make a unilateral decision that affects the lives of other individuals without offering them a voice in that decision.

Just as there are ways of getting compliance *to* change, there are many ways of getting cooperation *with* change. In fact, some of the techniques for gaining cooperation are quite simple and can be easily used to implement simpler changes that require only compliance.

We have already discussed several aspects of group dynamics that support change. How you have people working on the change is as important to its successful implementation as what the change is. That is, personal involvement is as much a function of the change *process* as it is of the change content.

This chapter discusses four simple, time-tested techniques that will maximize the probability of getting better group involvement. They are: brainstorming, consensus decision making, force-field analysis, and cause-and-effect analysis. What makes these methods so powerful is that they are simple and easy to control and they maximally involve the participants in the change process.

BRAINSTORMING

The process of brainstorming is designed to marshall group energy in a "stream of conscious creativity." Although we are all creative to varying degrees, we all seem to have a tendency, at times, to stifle our own creativity when working alone and to stifle others' creativity when working in groups.

Human creativity operates on a continuum, just like any other human capacity. On one side of the polarity is the "creative genius" who comes up with wildly imaginative ideas. On the other side of the polarity is the "logical censor," whose job it is to make sure that everything is safe and works just right. The thrust is toward self-monitoring and being sure that one never makes a mistake.

Both sides provide important capacities that are essential to the group's success. The problem is that they tend to trip over each other. While the creative genius is shouting, "What a great idea!," the logical censor is saying, "It'll never work." The usual result is that the idea is shut down before it has had a chance to be examined and developed.

The process of brainstorming allows the creative side to work unleashed, so that more imaginative and nontraditional approaches to problems and changes have a chance to surface. The objective of brainstorming is to come up with as many ideas as possible. The assumption is that if the quantity is there, so will be the quality.

There are two basic methods of brainstorming: free wheeling and nominal group technique.

Free Wheeling

Free wheeling brainstorming is a high-energy process that can be compared to popping corn. When you put the kernels in the corn popper and plug it in, there is a bit of time when the kernels just sit there as the heat increases. Then the kernels begin to explode at a rapid and unpredictable rate. This is what free wheeling brainstorming does in terms of producing ideas.

The issue to be dealt with could be any one of many (e.g., "How do we implement this change?," "What do we have to consider when thinking about this change?," or "What is contributing to the need for change?"). Regardless of the specific topic, you want to get as many different views as you can, with the maximum number of people participating. The objective of brainstorming is to generate as many ideas as possible. The premise is that the more unrestricted ideas there are, the higher the probability that there will be some of value.

The procedure for free wheeling brainstorming is as follows:

1. The change leader reviews the guidelines for brainstorming and states the topic or problem.

2. The participants generate ideas freely and as they think of them. The rules for this step are as follows:

   a. No criticism or evaluation of ideas is permitted while they are being generated.
   b. Wild ideas are welcomed.
   c. Quantity of ideas is stressed over quality at this point.
   d. It is fine to combine with and build on the ideas of others.

3. A recorder writes each idea on a flip chart, as it is stated, without editing.

4. When the participants have run out of new ideas, the ideas that have been recorded are clarified.

5. Duplicate ideas are combined.

6. Each idea is examined and discussed. A decision is made to keep, refine, or discard the idea.

7. A new list of workable ideas is the product.

Although free wheeling is the most common form of brainstorming, it has a few disadvantages. First, there is usually a wide range of personal styles in a work group. Some people speak more freely or are louder than others. The tendency is for the more outgoing people to develop a rhythm in generating ideas. This risks losing the input of the quieter, more contemplative members.

A second problem is that if the change leader does not stay in control of the process, it can lose focus. Attempts to bring it back, while essential, can interrupt the creative flow. To deal with these concerns, a second type of brainstorming is used: the nominal group technique (NGT).

Nominal Group Technique

The procedure for NGT is as follows:

1. The change leader reviews the guidelines for NGT and states the task.

2. *Silent Generation of Ideas.* Instead of immediately moving into an expression of ideas, the group members maintain silence for three-to-five minutes, while they individually write down as many ideas as they can in response to the task.

3. *Serial Collection of Ideas.* The rules for this step are as follows:

    a. One idea is expressed per turn, per person. The change leader polls each group member, in turn, to solicit one idea from each person. Any attempt by a group member to give a second idea on a round is gently stopped by the change leader. When the last group member is polled, the change leader goes back to the first member polled to get a second idea, and a new round begins.
    b. It is all right to pass and reenter at any time. It is highly unlikely that many group members will come up with the same number of ideas during the silent generation. Also, there is a high probability that there will be some duplication of ideas on different members' lists. If a group member runs out of ideas and chooses to pass on a round, he or she can reenter on the next round if something triggers a new idea.
    c. No comments or criticism of ideas is permitted. The goal is still to develop as many new and creative ideas as possible, although at a more controlled pace.

4. A recorder writes each idea on a flip chart, as it is stated, with no editing.

5. At the very end of the serial collection, a five-minute free wheeling session can be initiated to capture the last ideas.

NGT has three distinct advantages over free wheeling. First, it assures that all group members have equal opportunity in the brainstorming process. Because the rules are agreed on beforehand, there is little risk of alienating the more vocal group members in the attempt to get more participation from the quiet people in the group.

THE CHANGE LEADER

Second, the NGT process yields a much greater number of ideas than does free wheeling. Although there might be fewer ideas from a specific individual, getting everyone to contribute fully usually more than makes up for this. There also seems to be some advantage in having members be a little more contemplative in initiating the process by silently thinking about what would work.

Finally, NGT provides the change leader with control of the process. If there is a time crunch, or if an immediate response to a change is needed, the change leader can modify the instructions to respond to the situation. For example, the change leader could say, "We're going to have a three-minute period of silent generation of ideas and then two rounds of suggestions. I'd like your two best ideas."

There are no hard rules about when to use free wheeling brainstorming or when to use the nominal group technique. If you want a short, high-energy session that encourages thinking "outside the box," a free wheeling session would be most appropriate. On the other hand, if you are looking for a higher yield of ideas directed toward a specific outcome, NGT would probably work better.

CONSENSUS DECISION MAKING

The quality of decisions and the commitment to them is based in large part on how individuals and groups make the decisions. There are numerous decision-making processes, all of which have the potential to yield the best results under the proper circumstances. Some of them are as follows.

The Unilateral Decision. This is the simplest process. The person in charge makes the decision for the group, and the group is obligated to carry it out.

Minority Rule. A committee or an influential subgroup has the authority to decide for the entire group.

Majority Rule. The entire group votes on the issue, and the majority view dominates over the minority opinion.

Consensus. In this process, there is no minority dissention because everyone agrees to support the selected option to some degree.

Unanimous Consent. Everyone in the group agrees that a particular option is the best possible choice.

When working with change, the more you can obtain consensus in the group, the higher the probability that you will obtain optimal commitment to the decision.

Guidelines for Consensus Seeking

To achieve consensus, the following guidelines must be in place and agreed on *by consensus* before the decision-making process begins.

1. Any group member can say whatever he or she wants, as often as necessary.

2. Differences of opinion are viewed as natural and helpful.

3. Conflict-reducing techniques such as averaging, voting, or trading are not permitted.

4. There is a commitment to stay with the process until a supportable option is agreed on or a deadlock occurs.

5. No option is selected over anyone's objection.

Consensus has been reached when three conditions exist:

1. Each group member has had an opportunity to state his or her opinion and is satisfied that his or her position is understood by the entire group.

2. Everyone believes that he or she understands the opinions of all other group members.

3. Each member agrees to support the selected decision, whether or not he or she prefers it to others.

Consensus is—by far—the preferred decision-making strategy for developing creative processes for change and commitment to them. However, it is important not make a religion out of consensus. Although it may be the preferred approach in most cases, it is by no means the only approach. In order to maintain a balanced view, consider the following.

Consensus Versus Unanimous Consent

In considering the choices available for decision making, it is important to distinguish between consensus and unanimous consent. Consensus seeking is often a time-consuming and difficult process, although there is almost always the possibility of it.

What characterizes consensus most clearly is that everyone supports the final decision *to some degree*. Although there is no disagreement, there can be a very wide range of agreement. Some members may enthusiastically support a specific option while others feel that a better choice could have been made, but they agree to go along. So long as there is no objection to the selected option, you have consensus.

With unanimous consent, every group member agrees that the chosen option is the best possible under the circumstances. Unanimous consent is infinitely more difficult to reach than consensus and it is almost always unnecessary in dealing with organizational problems. The only time that unanimous consent is appropriate is when the issue is of critical concern and there is little or no margin for error. The most common example of an appropriate use of unanimous consent is trial by jury.

Don't Assume Consensus

What may happen, particularly during a hard-fought session, is that eventually what seems to be a mutually acceptable option will emerge. The change leader states the option and asks the group, "Is there anyone here who cannot support this solution?" The change leader is met with silence and assumes that consensus has been reached—which may not be the case.

Granted, every group member must take full responsibility for his or her silence. Nevertheless, you—as the change leader—are on much more solid ground if you poll the group for responses. Each member of the group needs to publicly state that he or she supports the proposed solution before consensus is achieved. Not only does this place the responsibility for the decision where it belongs, on each individual member, it also reinforces individual commitment to the decision.

Consensus Is Not Always Available

Sometimes, reaching consensus is not possible. The group may be too emotionally divided on an issue; the change may be totally unacceptable to almost everyone; or the group may be polarized because some of the guidelines for consensus have been violated. As the change leader, you have several ways to respond to the situation. If you sense from the beginning that consensus is going be difficult or impossible to reach, you can say to the group, "This is going to be a tough one; if we cannot reach clear consensus in thirty minutes, how about if we go to a majority vote?" If you have this procedure agreed to by consensus, at least you will have some commitment to the outcome and an easier time dealing with conflict issues. Another choice is simply to use another decision-making method from the beginning.

Paired Comparisons

Sometimes consensus is difficult to reach because the variables have become unwieldy: there are too many choices to consider, there are too many people involved in the process, or there is a very tight time schedule. Paired-comparison decision making is one quick and controlled way to test for consensus early. This method compares every option with every other option to discover what the group members think is important and what the best choice is of those available.

For example, a group that is discussing a change has used NGT to produce suggestions for implementation. After discussing the suggestions and combining similar suggestions, the group has reduced the list to six very acceptable options. The group now has to decide which option it will implement and support. The change leader chooses to use a paired-comparison process and takes the group through the following steps.

1. *Each suggestion is posted, clarified, and assigned a number.* The change leader or the group recorder writes the first suggestion on a clean flip-chart sheet. The group is asked if the suggestion is clear. If it is, it is designated suggestion #1. The second suggestion is dealt with in the same way and is designated suggestion #2. This process is continued until all the suggestions are clarified and given numbers.

2. *Each group member individually compares every choice with every other choice.* When all the suggestions are clear and posted, each group member creates a matrix, as illustrated below, on a clean piece of paper.

CHOICES					**TOTALS**
1/2	**1/3**	**1/4**	**1/5**	**1/6**	**1 =**
	2/3	**2/4**	**2/5**	**2/6**	**2 =**
		3/4	**3/5**	**3/6**	**3 =**
			4/5	**4/6**	**4 =**
				5/6	**5 =**
					6 =

Beginning with the first row, each member individually compares suggestion #1 with suggestion #2 and circles the choice. Then suggestion #1 is compared with suggestion #3, and, again, the choice is circled, and so forth until suggestion #1 has been compared to every other suggestion and a choice for each has been made. This process repeats, comparing suggestion #2 with every other suggestion, and so forth until every comparison has been made. Then each member totals the number of circles for each choice and writes the total in the column on the right.

3. *The group choice is calculated.* When everyone has completed the task, the change leader polls the group and gets a total number for how many times each suggestion was chosen.

If one option has accumulated a significant amount of circles over all the others, a consensus may have been reached. Even if this occurs, however, do not take the consensus for granted. Ask the group if there is, in fact, a consensus.

In many cases this process will narrow the options to two or three that are very close. This makes it much easier to attempt to reach consensus. On the other hand, if time has run out and a decision is needed, you can probably select the suggestion most frequently chosen by the group and receive minimum resistance.

Triage

Although not having enough reasonable choices is frequently seen as the main block to effective decision making and problem solving, having too many options is almost as bad. When energy and creativity are high, the group may generate so many options that it either doesn't know how to deal with them or it bogs down in trying to identify the ones that are worthy of consideration.

A helpful way of dealing with this problem is called "triage." It originated in World War I. Because of the heavy casualty rate, a method was needed to diagnose the condition of wounded soldiers rapidly so that the limited medical resources could be used to best advantage. Three categories were created: (1) walking wounded (those who had superficial or non-life-threatening injuries); (2) seriously wounded (those whose injuries were life threatening but who might be saved); and (3) terminally wounded (those who clearly would die from their injuries). When large numbers of wounded soldiers came in, nurses could quickly place the injured soldiers in the appropriate categories. Then the seriously wounded were attended to first, the walking wounded second, and the terminally wounded were made as comfortable as possible and set aside.

The triage method of prioritizing works well as a means of making quick judgments concerning the acceptability of alternatives. As with the medical example, three categories are created for suggestions. Any suggestions that cannot be placed immediately in one of the three categories are ignored. The three categories are as follows:

1. *No-brainers.* These are suggestions that will work and are easy to implement, e.g., move the broom locker fifty feet closer to the work area.

2. *Good ideas that can be implemented.* These are suggestions that will work but will take time and resources to implement, e.g., create a flex-time work schedule.

3. *Good ideas that cannot be implemented.* These are suggestions that will work but are outside the group's capacity to implement, e.g., change the company policy.

Once the triage is completed, category 1 ideas are simply assigned to someone to carry out, and the group moves on. Category 3 ideas are noted for possible future reference and then set aside. Category 2 ideas are put to a selection process to get consensus on which one(s) will be adopted by the group.

IDENTIFICATION STRATEGIES

One of the paradoxes on which this book is based is that the more complex the change, the simpler it is to implement. Many organizational changes are monolithic and are, therefore, very difficult to work with (e.g., a change in policy or in the organization's mission). If the change can be broken into smaller elements, there is a higher probability that more options can be developed for its implementation, *actively* involving more people. Two strategies that are excellent in destructuring large issues into more workable elements are force-field analysis and cause-and-effect analysis.

Force-Field Analysis

Force-field analysis (FFA) was developed by a social psychologist named Kurt Lewin (1974). It is a graphic process that allows the people working on a change to get a clear understanding of all the relevant factors.

Lewin suggested that every condition is as it is because there are forces in the environment pushing to make it happen and, at the same time, an equal number of forces pushing to block it.

To plan to implement a change with the best outcome and least resistance, you need to take a look at the factors under your control that impede or support group involvement, implementation of the change, and accep-

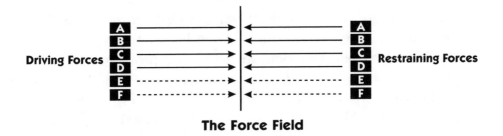

The Force Field

tance of the change. When the group is considering options, force-field analysis can be used to analyze them.

The forces pushing for a change are called *driving forces,* and the forces working against the change are called *restraining forces.* For example, in considering whether to change one's route to work, a driving force (for the change) might be that the original route now is full of potholes, and a restraining force (against the change) might be that the alternative route takes more time.

Once the nature of each force is identified, a choice can be made to either increase a driving force or decrease a restraining force, either of which will move the situation toward change.

To illustrate, suppose that tardiness has risen to 12 percent across the organization, and upper management is demanding that it not exceed 7 percent. One way to attempt to change the situation is simply to make a policy statement that "Being late three times in any twenty-day period will result in a one-day layoff without pay." Believe it or not, there are some organizations that do things this way! The attempt is to scare people into compliance. The actual change is most likely to be from "don't be late" to "don't get caught being late."

In a more cooperative approach, the change leader might prepare a basic force-field analysis chart and lead the group through the following procedure.

1. *The present condition is identified.* The existing condition is stated as specifically as possible. In this case, "tardiness has risen to 12 percent."

2. *The desired level is identified.* Again, as simply and as specifically as possible, the desired level is identified, in this case, "tardiness should not exceed 7 percent." The goal is not stated as 0 percent because that is not likely to be achieved and would not be worth the investment if it were. One of the most important aspects of facilitating change is to make sure that the change is meaningful and achievable in everybody's view.

3. *The group brainstorms a list of all the restraining forces.* Using the nominal group technique, the change leader has the group identify all the factors that are contributing to the problem of tardiness (or against a change for the better). Some of these might be: poor road conditions, snow storms, low morale, poor supervision, or inadequate parking. The restraining forces are entered on the chart.

4. *Using NGT, the group brainstorms a list of all the driving forces—those that are pushing toward lowering the rate of tardiness.* These might be improved working conditions, high unemployment rates in the area, the opportunity to work overtime, good supervision, or challenging work. The driving forces are entered on the chart.

5. *The forces are characterized.* One way to get a sharper image of the situation is to characterize each arrow that represents a driving or a restraining force, after they have all been identified. What you are looking for is an approximately equal amount of "arrow" on both sides of the line.

   a. You can alter the length of the arrow to indicate how long the particular force has been a factor. For example:

   Up to 90 days

   90 days to one year

   Over one year

   b. You also can vary the thickness of the arrow to indicate how important the force is. For example:

   Little impact

   Moderate impact

   Heavy impact

   c. By consensus, you can have the group judge the length and impact of each factor.

6. *The group selects a strategy.* The group can now decide if it wants to work with a force that is easy, in order to push a quick change, or to work with a more difficult force that will yield a bigger change. It also needs to decide whether it wants to increase a driving force or decrease a restraining force. There are no firm rules regarding this, but all things being equal, you are almost always better off attempt-

ing to reduce a restraining force than you are attempting to increase a driving force.

a. Reducing a restraining force. Attempting to reduce a restraining force by finding out what is contributing to the tardiness and responding to it has high probability of being effective. It also affords the opportunity to include the workers in the process of change.

b. Increasing a driving force. When a driving force is perceived as positive by the workers, increasing it is a smart strategy. It is bound to get a lot of support. However, when a driving force is perceived as negative by the workers (e.g., "pressure from management"), when you increase it, a new restraining force often arises to meet it, and you are still in equilibrium.

In the example of attempting to reduce tardiness, installing a time clock would be increasing a driving force. If you did this, the chances are that it would be greatly resented. Some employees even might begin to punch their friends' time cards, if the friends were late. This would create a new, more serious, restraining force. This takes us back to the primary theme of the book. In arbitrarily installing a time clock, you would be making a decision that affects the workers without including them in the decision.

7. *The group chooses the force.* A consensus-seeking procedure is used to select one or two forces that can be modified by the group to support the desired change. Appropriate action plans are then developed.

In working with change, force-field analysis has three distinct benefits. First, it provides a pictorial representation of the issues surrounding the change. Second, it breaks the change situation into very simple and clearly defined elements that are easier to work with. Third, it provides an overall, balanced view of the demand for change. The group can look at what is working for the change and against the change, at what has gone wrong and what has gone right. This balanced view can do a lot to reduce resistance to the change and keep the group focused on working with the present situation.

Cause-and-Effect Analysis

Cause-and-effect analysis is another process that is quite effective in breaking simple changes into more complex and workable elements. Sometimes know as a "fishbone diagram" or Ishikawa (1972) diagram (after the person who originated it), a cause-and-effect analysis is an alternative to force-field analysis. Instead of looking at driving and restraining forces, it looks at categories of causes. This can be used to analyze a situation, problem, or change. Using the example of tardiness, let us walk through a cause-and-effect analysis.

1. *The present condition is identified.* In this case, tardiness has risen to 12 percent across the organization.

2. *The categories of cause are identified.* The task now is to identify the organizational categories that could be housing the cause for the change. Typical organizational categories are "Materials," "Methods," "Machines," "Policy," "Management," "Manpower," and so forth. The relevant categories are placed in a "fishbone" diagram as shown in the following figure. The need for change is in the "head" position.

3. *The group brainstorms possible causes for the change using free wheeling brainstorming.* The recorder places each idea under one of the categories. This is usually done at the suggestion of the contributor; the recorder can check with the group to see if the category makes sense.

4. *The group identifies the most likely causes.* When all ideas have been generated and categorized, the group, by consensus, selects the one or two most likely causes of the need for change.

5. *The group verifies the most likely cause.* Something is done to verify the cause so that some action can be taken to facilitate the change.

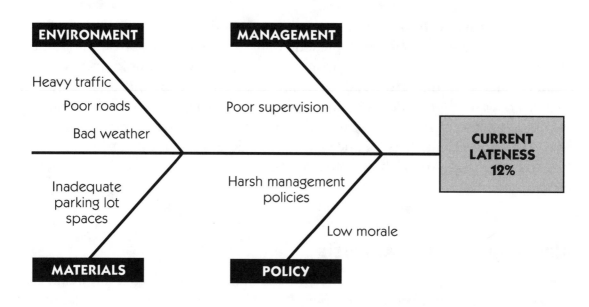

Cause-and-Effect Analysis

For example, if "low morale" is identified as the most prominent cause of tardiness, the human resources department can be approached to see if it would support a random survey to determine if this is indeed the case. Once a cause is verified, appropriate action plans can be developed.

These group techniques discussed in this chapter are by no means the only ones available. A lot of problem-solving and decision-making methods can be used in creating positive change in an organization. So long as the technique involves the people who will be affected and maximizes their opportunity to have input in the implementation, any technique is as good as any other. The ones described here, however, are enough to get you started.

References

Ishikawa, K. (1972). *Guide to quality control.* Asian Productivity Organization.

Lewin, K. (1974, June). Frontiers in group dynamics, concepts, methods, and reality in social science. *Human Relations, 1,* pp. 5-42.

GROUP ACTIVITY: PRIORITY WORKSHEET
Concept/Objectives

It is a good idea to have several group techniques available for each problem-solving or decision-making function so that the group does not become bored with or locked into the change process. An optional means of selecting a specific problem or solution, after a triage of positive ideas, is the priority worksheet.

Directions:

1. After a brainstorming session to generate ideas, use triage to get the options down to four-to-seven ideas, each of which has real potential.

2. Using consensus, develop a list of five or six criteria that are relevant in making the decision, e.g., cost, acceptability by upper management, complexity.

3. Rank the criteria and list them across the top of the page in rank order.

4. List the specific suggestions from the triage down the side of the page.

5. Have each group member individually rate each suggestion in terms of each criterion and total the response for each suggestion under the Total column on the right side of the page.

6. Accumulate the ratings from the entire group for each suggestion.

7. Based on a group discussion of the results, attempt to reach consensus on the specific option to be adopted by the group.

PRIORITY WORKSHEET								
PROBLEMS OR OPPOR-TUNITIES	**IMPORTANCE** 5-Important, Pressure 4- 3-Some Concern 2- 1-LIttle Concern	**RESOURCES NEEDED** 5-Modest 4- 3-Considerable 2- 1-Large Amount	**AUTHORITY** 5-Leader 4- 3-Two Levels 2- 1-Several Levels	**COMPLEXITY** 5-Not Complex 4- 3-Modest Complexity 2- 1-Complex	**TIME TO IMPLEMENT** 5-Month or Less 4- 3-Three Months 2- 1-Six Months or More	**RESULTS** 5-Measurable 4- 3-Some Indicators 2- 1-Intangible	**OTHER** 5- 4- 3- 2- 1-	**TOTAL** Sum the Ratings

CHAPTER**SIX**

Working with Resistance

One of the most difficult aspects of managing change is trying to overcome the resistance that is almost always associated with it. Resistance to change is considered by many to be part of human nature. This view is understandable but not necessarily correct. Although there frequently is an association between change and resistance, it is not necessarily the cause-and-effect relationship that people assume.

How resistance is viewed and managed is a critical aspect of the change process. Most approaches to managing change view resistance as a natural, negative result of any attempt to implement change. In this view, resistance must be overcome and eliminated. I think resistance needs to be honored and worked with. This positive view of resistance can be explained by examining resistance by itself and then looked at within the context of the change process.

DEFINITION OF RESISTANCE

Many large organizations have clearly stated values that place high significance on things such as openness and trust, team development, and cooperation and collaboration. Unfortunately, if cooperation is seen as good, resistance—almost by definition—is seen as bad. This judgment is just as dysfunctional as saying that if change is good, maintaining the status quo is bad, or if collaboration is good, competition is bad. The reality is that every human capacity has a potential for being either good or bad, depending on the circumstances in which it occurs. Resistance is the same.

Although most people define resistance within the context of change, I suggest that although it may occur within the change process, its origin is in the context of power.

Earlier, I defined power as the ability to get all of what you want from the environment, given what's available. Keeping that in mind, we can define resistance as *the ability to avoid what you don't want from the environment*. The relationship between the two can be seen in the figure that follows.

	I want	I don't want
I get	**POWER** (+)	**VICTIM** (-)
I don't get	**LOSER** (-)	**RESISTANCE** (+)

Power and Resistance Model

In the figure there are four possibilities. I either want something or I don't want it; then I either get that thing or I don't get it. Power is a means to an end, not an end in itself, and resistance operates exactly the same way.

Looking at the upper left quadrant in the figure, the condition is that I want something and I get it. This is power, and most people would agree that getting what you want is a positive condition. Looking at the lower left quadrant, I don't want something and I manage to avoid it. Avoiding what I don't want is as good as getting what I do want. This is resistance. For example, getting out of having to do the dishes (resistance) is as much to my benefit as getting to go to the movies (power).

THE CHANGE LEADER

There are two negative conditions in the model. In the upper right quadrant, I get something I don't want, which I describe as being a victim. In the lower left quadrant, I want something but I don't get it, which is being a loser. The obvious strategy is to expand the positive areas and decrease the negative ones.

Thus, resistance is not negative; it is positive. It is important that we stop telling ourselves and others to stop being resistant.

How Resistance Works:
The Topdog-Underdog Continuum

Think about the last time you made a New Year's resolution. Did you keep it? Like many older adults, I have stopped making them because I didn't keep most of them.

Going back to the premise that all human characteristics operate in polarities, one salient dimension is topdog/underdog. This is what stops most people from sticking to their New Year's resolutions and other self-help programs.

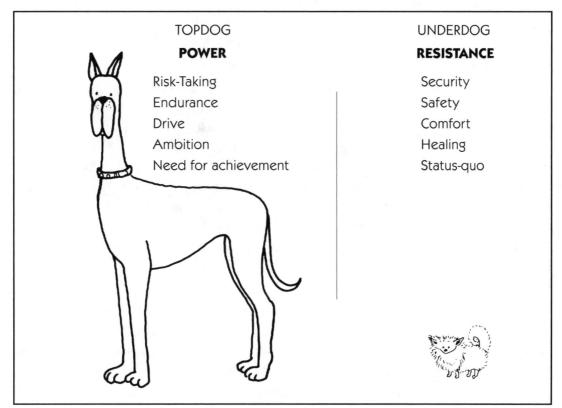

TOPDOG	UNDERDOG
POWER	**RESISTANCE**
Risk-Taking	Security
Endurance	Safety
Drive	Comfort
Ambition	Healing
Need for achievement	Status-quo

The Topdog/Underdog Continuum

The topdog is the part of you that houses power. It contains all the capacities for getting you what you want, i.e., endurance, drive, ambition, risk taking, and the need for achievement (change). All the self-improvement needs (e.g., stop smoking, lose fifteen pounds, earn another degree) are housed within the topdog.

The underdog is that part of you that houses resistance. Its function is to keep you safe and alive. It is made up of characteristics such as the needs for safety, comfort, healing, security, and the desire for the status quo.

It's the topdog that sets you on the road to success with a big bon voyage party, and it's the underdog that consistently messes up the trip. For example, you resolve to lose fifteen pounds, but make the resolution two weeks before going on vacation. You promise to be more understanding with your employees, but wait until the last minute to state your dissatisfaction with what has been done.

As soon as the failure occurs, there is a rush of guilt and self-contempt and a firmer resolve to beat the problem the next time. This continues; eventually you admit defeat.

After you break a resolution to improve yourself, the tendency is for the topdog to try to kill the underdog. Even though the topdog is characterized by drive, endurance, and ambition, and the underdog is characterized by the need for safety and comfort, if the conflict goes on long enough, the underdog always wins!

As with any human characteristic, the topdog/underdog subboundary describes how much capacity you have for pursuing what you want versus how much risk you are willing to take. The topdog is that part of you that gets you where you are going, but it's your underdog who keeps you alive in the process. Your underdog stops you from taking on too much, from overreaching your capabilities, and from committing yourself to things that are not in your best interest. It's also critical in keeping you alive in threatening situations. For example, its your topdog that vows to take no more guff from your boss in staff meetings, and it's your underdog that slams your larynx shut just before you tell the boss off and commit organizational suicide.

People whose topdogs have temporarily vanquished their underdogs are headed for disaster. Such people take any risk regardless of the cost, confront every issue regardless of its importance, go head-to-head with every person regardless of position, and tend to see themselves as immortal. You don't see many people like this in organizations today because they either self-destruct or the organization gets rid of them.

Unfortunately, people whose underdogs have killed their topdogs abound in organizations. Such people take no risks, have no opinions that do not reflect the majority view, volunteer for nothing, and leave no indication of whether they were there last week or not.

It is important to realize that you need both topdog and underdog attributes to be effective. Instead of having them constantly at war with each other, the trick is to integrate them and have them work together. For example, instead of swearing to lose fifteen pounds, lose five pounds and then decide if you want to lose another five or not. Rather than either swallowing abuse or publicly confronting your boss, find a time to let him or her know privately how you feel and that you would like to explore ways to make the relationship better for both of you.

Resistance As a Personal Asset

When people resist a change—particularly one that looks good to you—your safest assumption is that people are not being perverse or responding without thinking, they are simply protecting themselves.

The main purpose of resistance is to protect. You are going to resist things that you see as being potentially harmful to you, no matter who says that you should or should not, including yourself. Resistance keeps you from getting hurt, it guards your effectiveness, it heightens your awareness of yourself, and it keeps you from becoming distracted.

Resistance Keeps You from Getting Hurt

Two of the assumptions that this perspective is based on were mentioned earlier:

- people don't resist change, they resist pain; and
- one of the most painful things there is is boredom, which is the opposite of change.

Your resistance stops you from rushing headlong into situations that are potentially harmful to you. In some cases you are aware of the potential danger and consciously back away from it. For example, this is what keeps most of us from sky diving, alligator wrestling, and insulting traffic policemen who have just pulled us over.

In other cases the resistance stems from a hunch or a gut reaction. Such reactions often tell us that something isn't right, even if we don't know exactly what it is. At the very minimum, we should refuse to make a personal commitment until we know more—or feel better—about the change.

Resistance Guards Your Effectiveness

One well-established assumption from the behavioral sciences is that most people display a need for growth and challenge. Supportive of this is the view that people need to avoid failure as much as they need to succeed. This suggests that most people will gladly take on new challenges that are risky but have a reasonable chance for success. On the other hand, as the difficulty of the challenge increases, so does the chance of failure. The accompanying resistance to the change increases at about the same rate.

Your topdog shouts "Yes" to every challenge, regardless of its chance of failure. Your underdog whimpers "No" to every challenge, regardless of its chance of success. You need an integrated response that allows you to take on the toughest challenge that you can that does not exceed your current capabilities. For example, a high jumper might attempt a new personal record that exceeds his best jump by two inches, not by two feet.

As a change leader, your safest assumption is that when your employees are resisting a change, they are not trying to block you or cause problems, they are guarding their own effectiveness. It doesn't cost much to at least listen to what they are saying.

Resistance Heightens Your Awareness of Yourself

I do not go around maintaining an awareness of myself and I know very few people who do. (Those who do usually are incredible bores.) The times that I am most aware of who I am is when I have a difficult choice to make that causes me to weigh potential outcomes. It is hard not be aware of yourself in such a situation because you are weighing your personal values, which is probably your most identifying set of characteristics. I am most aware of my values and what is important to me when everyone else is shouting "Yes" and I am gritting my teeth and saying "No."

Until you understand your own resistance to the change and honor it as being natural and appropriate, you are not going to be respectful of the resistance of others. When individuals are resisting the change you are trying to implement, they are giving you clear messages about who they are and what's important to them. If you listen, you will be able to identify and work with the issues that are causing them concern.

Resistance Keeps You from Becoming Distracted

One of the most beneficial functions of resistance is that it allows you to focus on a specific target. For example, if you were not resisting right now, it would be practically impossible to read and understand these words. A truck would go by and you'd listen to the sound; a fly would enter the room and you would visually follow its flight; or a word would remind you of someone's name and you'd be off reminiscing. Your resistance allows you to block out most extraneous stimuli so as to fully concentrate on what you are doing.

Resistance As an Organizational Asset

Just as resistance is advantageous to individuals, it is beneficial to organizations. It differentiates talent; it provides new information; it produces energy; and it makes the work environment safe.

Resistance Differentiates Talent

One assumption of the Gestalt approach to human development is that behind every "no" is a "yes." As is mentioned earlier, people will go to great lengths to resist challenges and changes that have a high probability of ending up in personal failure. When you, as a change leader, are being blocked because someone is telling you "No" through resistant behavior, rather than insisting on change, you would do better to find out what the person would rather do. Most people will be happy to tell you what they are really good at and where they think they could make their best contributions. The more you can identify and tap these areas, the more talent you bring to the change process with minimal resistance.

Most of your employees probably realize that you can't accommodate everyone all the time in bringing about needed change. Knowing that you are ready to give them their preferences when possible will help them to reduce needless resistance when the situation demands that they work in their least-favorite ways.

Resistance Provides New Information

On the assumption that your people are not just out to give you a bad time, when people resist something, it's safe to assume that they see things differently from you. Each different perspective is a vital source of information that could be critical in making the change work.

It is as important for you as it is for your employees to have them express their views. They may or may not ultimately influence the change but, either way, everyone is better informed by having all views expressed.

Resistance Produces Energy

Human energy is as vital to running an organization as gasoline is to running an automobile. Autos can coast for quite a distance, and so can most organizations. For an organization to maintain its vitality and growth, however, it must have a base of energy, excitement, and activity. One source of this energy is the organization's active pursuit of its goals and objectives; a second source is the organization's sense of humor; and the third and deepest source is how openly and directly the organization honors and works with conflict and resistance.

For example, both a relay race and a tug-of-war have an objective to be met, concerted team effort is involved, and there is a clear indicator of success or failure. The most salient factor that the two events share is that they both produce energy, one from a power strategy (pursuing an objective) and the other from a strategy of resistance (avoiding being dragged through mud). The only difference between the two events is that in the relay race the energy is focused on advancing, whereas in the tug-of-war the energy is focused on "pulling back." The critical factor is to get the energy surfaced. (I most aware of my energy when I am being dragged off, kicking and screaming, to a place I would prefer not to go.) Once the energy is recognized, it becomes a relatively simple task to channel it in a productive direction.

Resistance Makes the Work Environment Safe

Whenever anyone says to me, "Don't be so defensive," my reflexive response is, "You stop attacking and I'll stop defending!" As we know, people will defend themselves and resist things perceived as harmful no matter who says they shouldn't. When you establish a norm that honors this human reaction, self-protection becomes a value, and the work environment becomes a lot more safe. The irony is that as the work environment becomes increasingly safer, there is much less need for resistance.

DEALING WITH RESISTANCE

Unfortunately, because resistance has been so devalued, most change leaders use three low-yield strategies to try to overcome it. These strategies are as follows.

Breaking Resistance Down. The first strategy is an attempt to break resistance down. This is typified by such tactics as the use of threat or coercion, trying to "sell" the change, or an appeal to reason (e.g., "If you only understood why I want this change, the logic would be inescapable").

Avoiding Resistance. The second strategy is an attempt to avoid resistance. Examples of this are "not hearing" the resistance, deflecting the resistance (e.g., "Yes, but..."), and inflicting guilt.

Minimizing Resistance. The third dysfunctional strategy is an attempt to minimize resistance. Typical tactics are discounting the resistance as unimportant, calling on tradition, and maintaining that unanimity is more important than the issue at hand.

Although these low-yield strategies do work to some degree, in that they may obtain a temporary positive response from the resistor, there are two problems that result from all of them.

The first problem is that they all leave the resistance basically untouched. All the emphasis is on selling the positive aspects of the change and on attacking the resistance as soon as it surfaces. The problem is that if you are successful in doing this, you don't get rid of the resistance that is there, you merely drive it underground. You have done nothing to respond to it, and now it is much harder to get to. You can be relatively sure that it will be back "to bite you" later.

The second problem is that in employing some of the tactics mentioned above—coercion, threat, and inflicting guilt—you increase the resistance, not only to the specific demand for change but to you and to the whole process of change. Of course, in most cases you can force compliance; however, *you can never force cooperation*. One of my favorite posters says, "Just because you have silenced a man, don't think you have converted him."

The Positive Approach to Resistance

The following two assumptions underlie the positive approach to resistance:

1. Resistance is a positive force and needs to honored rather than suppressed, avoided, or minimized.

2. The resistance is there; the only choice you have is whether to surface it or leave it buried. You are always better off having it surfaced.

This approach for working with resistance consists of an essential precondition and a four-step strategy. The steps are: surfacing, honoring, exploring, and rechecking. Each step must be completed before you move on to the next one.

Precondition

Be clear and concise about what you want from the resistors. This precondition is absolutely essential if the change is going to be implemented successfully. The surfacing of the resistance can be no clearer than the demand for change to which it is directed. You must be specific. The more you describe the change in terms of time frames, specific outcomes, and the concrete behaviors that will be needed to implement it, the higher the probability that the resistance will be clear and more easily workable.

This is the time to sell the change and put it in its best possible light. You want to highlight all the positive aspects of the change, both for the organization and for the individuals involved. This is the time to emphasize what's in it for them. A hard sell is all right in this phase. Once you move to working with the resistance, "selling" the change is no longer appropriate.

Step 1. Surface the Resistance

After you have stated clearly what you want in regard to the change and have answered all questions, your most difficult task is to get the resistance out into the open. Many people may initially hold back their resistance for any number of reasons. They may not trust your new approach; they may see themselves as being vulnerable; or they may not be clear themselves about their resistance. It is important for you to remember at this point that resistance is natural and self-protective. It can be worked with easily if you do two things.

Make It Safe. After you have stated and clarified the change that you want, point out that you realize that not everyone may see it the way you do. Point out that you need to hear the group members' opinions of the change and that no one is at risk for speaking honestly.

Ask for It All. It is not a pleasant experience to hear people tell you what's wrong with what you want. However, it is in your best interest to ask for and hear it all. It is all right to answer a question, but never use this as an opportunity to resell the change! Be sure to thank each person for his or her input; each is giving you what you asked for.

Step 2. Honor the Resistance

Listen. There is a time to listen and there is a time not to listen. This is definitely a time to listen! When someone is openly stating resistance, he or she is telling you two things that are very important. The first is vital information about what may not be workable in the change you want. The second is some clear statements about what is important to the person. It is crucial at this stage that you do nothing to reinforce your original demand; just listen.

Acknowledge the Resistance. Acknowledging the resistance is important because it lets the resistors know that they are being heard. Acknowledgment honors the others' concerns and their right to have them. You also honor the resistance by acknowledging that the intended change really could be a problem for *them*.

During this process, maintain eye contact, restate any important points that the resistor makes, and ask questions occasionally to increase clarity. Do not imply that you agree or disagree with the resistance, only that the resistor has a right to resist openly. Statements of acknowledgment, such as "I can see how this could be a problem for you" or "I wasn't aware of this aspect" or "I'm glad you have told me of this concern" help to create an empathic connection with the resistor but do not compromise your commitment to the change.

Reinforce the Right to Resist. As group members become more comfortable with this process and begin to trust that they are safe, the resistance will surface more easily. It is a good practice in the beginning to keep reinforcing the fact that they are safe in stating their resistance and that you appreciate their honesty. Saying "It's all right that you don't like all of this" or "I appreciate your being honest with me" will help to establish the process as a safe and effective way of dealing with change and the resistance to it.

Step 3. Explore the Resistance

Authentic and Pseudoresistance. Once the resistor feels safe and is willing to discuss the resistance openly, it is time to mutually explore the nature of the resistance. There are two types of resistance: authentic resistance and pseudoresistance.

Authentic resistance is directly focused on the change and has no objective other than to block or stop the change. Pseudoresistance has nothing to do with the change being demanded. It usually is grounded in experiences and attitudes that stem from the resistor's past. It originates in things such as resentment of authority, a general mistrust of people, a bad interpersonal relationship, or *not getting the recognition that one feels one deserves*. In my experience, the latter is a major cause of pseudoresistance. In any event, the resistance is being expressed against the demand for change but really has nothing to do with it.

Pseudoresistance can be dealt with fairly easily if you realize that it is occurring. The first indicator is that the resistor's statements are vague or general in nature, e.g., "I just don't think it will work" or "I just don't like it." You can respond to this with either of two questions: "It's really okay that you don't like it; what specifically is your objection?" or "What would you prefer?" The first question will force the resistor either to become specific in terms of his or her authentic resistance to the change or to back off. The second question also demands specificity; however, it is more positive and has the potential of creating some options. Actually, both questions can be used effectively in the above sequence.

Do not ask the resistor, "Why don't you like it?" The moment you introduce the word "why," you are demanding that the resistor justify or defend the resistance. This is guaranteed to increase the resistance and drive it underground.

If the resistance is pseudo, it will dissolve into some mumbling and end up as a face-saving grumble such as "Well, I still don't like it." Acknowledge that it is all right not to like it and shift your energy to the next person.

After the meeting, you might want to approach the pseudoresistor to inquire how things are going in general.

Probe. When the resistance has been identified as authentic, you can explore some ways to deal with it. For example, you can gently probe by responding with a statement such as, "I didn't realize that you had a time problem; is there something we can do to create more time for you?" or "I can see that you have a lot to deal with at the moment; is there some way we can reorganize your priorities to make this happen?" Anything that will move the resistor from a reactive to a proactive position is bound to help.

Step 4. Review

Most changes will require more than one meeting to initiate and implement. It is important that you keep written notes during this process. First, when you write down what people are saying, you are honoring their comments as being important. Second, you don't want to miss or forget any of the resistance that is brought out. If you do, you put your credibility at risk.

The last ten minutes of the change-group meeting should be devoted to a review of all the resistances that were stated and what, if anything, was agreed to about responding to them. For example, "Charlie, you were concerned that the proposed change wouldn't be fair to the newer members of the group. We agreed to check that out with the Human Resources Department." Or "Paula, you objected to the added time demands the change will make. I'm not sure what, if anything, we can do about that at the moment."

If the change is one that can be accomplished in a single meeting, the review allows for clean closure. If there is to be a second meeting, the review allows the work to be picked up at this point, rather than having to go back to the initial step.

Points to Consider

There May Still Be Some Resistance, and That's Okay. You probably aren't going to be able to eliminate all the resistance to a change, and that's okay. The objective of the positive strategy for working with resistance is not to remove all the resistance to the change, it is to remove the *needless* resistance to the change. People are still going to resist what they perceive as not in their best interests. However, any reduction in needless resistance will result in more cooperation with the change and less resentment. Usually this will be enough to allow you to go ahead with the change, confident that what you are seeing is what you are getting. That is, you can trust the level of positive response that you are getting and are at little risk of being "blindsided" later on.

Just Say "Thanks." When a resistor finally shrugs his or her shoulders and says, "Okay, let's try it and see what happens," there is a tendency to want to do something nice for the person. After all, he or she is willing to give to you some support for a change he or she still doesn't like. When this happens, I strongly suggest that you fight the urge to say something like, "I know that you'll really end up liking this" or "You'll be glad you came on board, once you get a chance to think about it." Although your intention will be to make it a positive change, your comment will sound patronizing, and the result is that you will increase whatever resistance you finally managed to reduce. All you need to do is recognize that it was the resistor's choice to go along with the change, and the only appropriate response is "Thank you."

SOME COMMON RESISTANCES AND CREATIVE COUNTERS

There are many ways in which resistance to change can be expressed, both verbally and behaviorally. Following are nine common expressions of resistance and their creative counters.

Resistance: The block.

Expression: "I don't want to" or "I'd rather not."

Comment: The block is the cleanest form of authentic resistance and the easiest with which to work. The resistor understands what the demander wants.

Counter: "What's your objection?"

Resistance: The rollover (passive resistance).

Expression: "Tell me *exactly* what you want me to do."

Comment: The rollover is one of the most difficult forms of resistance to identify and, therefore, one of the most difficult with which to work. Frequently, the resistor is not aware that he or she is resisting. Passive resistance is expressed by minimal compliance with the change and no compliance with the spirit of the change.

The most confounding aspect of passive resistance is that, at first, it looks as if you are getting compliance. However, when the person says, "Tell me exactly what you want me do in regard to this change," you had better tell that person *exactly*. If you fail to, you might later hear something like, "Well, you told me I had to wear the new safety glasses; you didn't say I had to wear them on my eyes!"

Counter: "Are you clear about what you are being asked to do and what constitutes good performance?" This forces the resistor to at least verbally acknowledge the spirit of the demand for change and to accept the responsibility for his or her choices regarding conformance.

Resistance: The stall.

Expression: "I'll get on it first thing next week."

Comment: It is sometimes difficult to tell the difference between a stall and an honest request for more time to complete a task. Knowing how the person usually responds to demands should help you to make the distinction.

Counter: "Is there anything of a serious nature that would prevent you from starting it tomorrow?"

Resistance: The reverse.

Expression: "Wow, what a *great* idea!"

Comment: The reverse is a very subtle form of resistance that is difficult to identify if you don't know the resistor well. It seems to be an enthusiastic statement of support when what you were expecting from this person was a hard time. Once the reverse is delivered, it is almost immediately followed by the stall. In effect, the resistor tells you what you want to hear, puts you off for a day, and then forgets about it.

Counter: "I am really pleased that you are so solidly behind this change. I'd like to hear all the specific things that you are feeling really positive about." Either the resistor will convince himself or herself while speaking that it is really a great idea or you will be able to see some suppressed gagging.

Resistance:	The sidestep.
Expression:	"Let Mikey try it."
Comment:	The appeal here is to your sense of fairness. The message is, "Why do we have to go along with this change when the people in building A don't have to?" If the resistor is successful, you will become defensive and attempt to justify your demand for change. Try to avoid this.
Counter:	"I appreciate your concern for the people in building A. I am aware of their situation and plan to respond to it. In the meantime, what I would like from you is...."

Resistance:	The projected threat.
Expression:	"The _____ isn't going to like this."
Comment:	The resistance is an implied threat that someone with more authority will not like or approve of the change you are implementing. The reality is that the person in authority may or may not approve. Either way, it is a separate issue and is not to be dealt with here.
Counter:	"I appreciate your concern and will check with the _____ later. What I'd like from you right now is...." Or, "I'll keep that in mind. Now, what objections do *you* have to the change?"

Resistance:	The press.
Expression:	"You owe me one."
Comment:	The press is an authentic resistance. In this case, the resistor does not want to support the change and is calling in an old debt to get off the hook. It might be a perfectly acceptable action to honor the resistance, as asked, and clear the books. The important thing is that it is *your decision* either way. If this is not the appropriate time to pay your debt, acknowledge that the debt exists but was incurred under other circumstances and that you would like the resistor to comply.
Counter:	"I realize that I owe you one; however, I need your help right now with this change. I will honor the debt at a more appropriate time."

Resistance:	The guilt trip.
Expression:	"See what you're making me do?"
Comment:	The use of guilt to shape behavior is a common and destructive tactic. Guilt is based on the erroneous assumption that we are always responsible for one another's welfare. Allowing for the occasional exception, a much sounder assumption is that of individual responsibility.
	"See what you are making me do" is an appeal to the change leader to disregard his or her own welfare in favor of the resistor's. The

	resistor's problem with what *you* want is *his or her problem,* not yours. It is wise to work with the problem but not to shoulder it.
Counter:	"I'm sorry that this is a problem for you; however, I'd like you to...." Or, "I recognize that you would prefer not to do this. I'll take full responsibility for demanding the change. Now, what I want you to do is...."

Resistance:	The tradition.
Expression:	"But we've always done it the other way."
Comment:	This form of resistance is probably the most common of them all. The traditional way of doing something should not be ignored simply because it is traditional. Sometimes the old way *is* the best way. More often than not, however, the appeal to tradition is an appeal for safety, not effectiveness. It is a strategy to ensure the status quo—even at the risk of mediocrity—because it is perceived as keeping risk and creativity to a minimum.
Counter:	"I understand the value of the traditional approach; however, I think that this situation is unique." Or, "I agree that the old approach has some merit. What could we do to adapt it to this situation?"

■ ■ ■

WORKING WITH EMERGING RESISTANCE

The techniques mentioned above all work very well with resistance that is expressed as protest to the demand for change. In many cases, however, resistance will first begin to surface as part of a positive or neutral discussion about the change. That is, both *you and the resistor* become aware of the resistance for the first time, at the same time. When this happens, the new resistance has not had time to incubate, and it is frequently too early, or the resistance too new, for it to be characterized. In this case, there are several things that you can do to maintain positive control of the conversation and the resistance at this early stage.

The most important thing is to fight the temptation to stomp the newly expressed resistance into the ground. If you attempt to do so, all you will succeed in doing is to drive the resistance underground where it can grow stronger. The way to deal with emerging resistance is simply to use the positive strategy discussed earlier in this chapter. The only difference is that instead of using it as a strategy, use it as a tactic. That is, rather than having a plan of action that you are following, simply stay in touch with the other person and *react* to the resistance.

The most effective tool at your disposal in this process is active listening. If the other person is convinced that his or her objections and concerns have been heard and will be responded to, you will increase his or her willingness to hear your position. Having this occur before the resistance hardens is your best chance of getting commitment to the change.

Active listening demonstrates that you are making a sincere attempt to maintain contact with the speaker and lets him or her know that you have actually heard what was said. Some effective active listening techniques are as follows:

■ ■ ■

Attending: To focus on the other person.
Examples: "I hear you." "I understand."

Encouraging: To convey your interest in listening.
Examples: "That's very interesting." "Tell me more."

Restating: To check your understanding or interpretation of the resistor's message.
Examples: "As I understand it, your concern is that...." "What you want me to do is...."

Reflecting: To demonstrate empathy for the speaker's position.
Examples: "You feel that...." "You're upset by the prospect of...."

Clarifying: To obtain additional data or to get the speaker to explore all sides of the demand for change.
Examples: "Is this the problem as you see it now?" "Do you mean that...?"

Summarizing: To bring the entire discussion into focus and to get closure for the moment.
Examples: "If I understand it, your major concern is...." "The big issues blocking your cooperation are...."

■ ■ ■

Active listening requires maintaining good eye contact with the speaker, a relaxed but attentive posture, and—most important of all—patience.

As you are listening, you can employ the steps of the positive strategy in response to the resistor's position. For example, "I appreciate your candor" makes it safe for the resistor. "I can appreciate your concern" acknowledges the resistor's position. Something like "Would doing it in sections help?" probes positive options with the resistor.

The main thing to keep in mind is that the resistance arose unexpectedly. When this happens, drop what you are doing and respond to it. Once it has been acknowledged and worked with, it is perfectly acceptable to go back to discussing the positive aspects of the change you desire.

WORKING WITH GROUP RESISTANCE

Resistance can occur in almost any setting and can be expressed by any creature with a central nervous system. Resistance is an individual phenomenon; each person can experience it only in his or her own way, no matter what the circumstances. Nevertheless, group dynamics can greatly influence individual resistance.

Most of us have experienced and observed the effect of group impact in lot of different ways. For example, having the "home court advantage" alludes to the fact that a cheering crowd can often make the difference in who wins a close game. On the negative and more dramatic side, peaceful demonstrators have turned into angry mobs with little provocation. Individual resistance also can be affected and escalated by a sense of group identity or common cause. This is a very difficult phenomenon to deal with, particularly if you are the sole advocate for a change and there is a groundswell of resistance rising against you.

There are several indicators that group resistance is starting to occur; if you can catch it in time, it is not that difficult to work with. Some of the indicative behaviors are as follows:

- The number and frequency of the statements of resistance noticeably increase.

- The nature of the resistance statements seems to be more pseudo than authentic.

- There is nonverbal communication among the resistors, e.g., nodding, eye contact, smiling, and so forth.

A group also can suddenly become passive-aggressive. Indicators of this are as follows:

- The group suddenly becomes silent.
- The members avoid eye contact with you.
- What is said is hostile and may even border on a personal challenge, e.g., "I don't know why we're even here" or "Just tell us what you want and let us out of here."

If you find yourself in this situation, there is a process that can help you work with the group and get you back in positive control.

1. Immediately state your awareness of what is happening and your discomfort with it. For example, you might say something like, "It seems to me that there are a number of people who are not happy

with what is happening here, including me. I think we need to address this so we can move on."

2. If you are working with more than seven group members, divide the total group into two or three equal subgroups.

3. Ask each member to individually write down a number, on a scale of one to seven, that represents his or her support for the proposed change. A one would indicate no support whatsoever; a seven would indicate total support.

4. Give the subgroups five minutes to brainstorm lists of everything they *don't* like about the change. Ask each subgroup to appoint a spokesperson and have that person write down every idea mentioned. Be sure to assure the group members that you really want to hear their lists and are not doing this to censor them.

5. At the end of five minutes, ask the spokesperson from the first group to read its list of objections. Maintain eye contact, question anything that is not clear, take notes when relevant, and thank the spokesperson when he or she is finished. Repeat this process with each subgroup.

6. When the last subgroup's spokesperson has announced its list, repeat step 4. This time ask the groups to list everything they *do* like about the proposed change. Then repeat step 5 to get the feedback.

7. When the feedback to you is finished, ask each member to write down a number from one to seven that indicates his or her support for the proposed change. When the members have done this, poll the entire group by asking for a show of hands as to how many people put down a lower number than they did the first time, how many put the same number as the first time, and how many put a higher number than they did the first time. There typically will be about a 20 percent increase in support for the change. You will then be able to continue working with the issue.

This technique is a way to get group process working for you rather than against you. If this fails to get the group in a mood to at least consider the merits of the change, your best bet is to end the meeting and tell the members that you need time to consider the situation. You need to find out what is blocking the process, because continuing under these conditions almost guarantees failure.

CHANGE-LEADER ACTIVITY: TOPDOG/UNDERDOG

Directions: Think of a change that you are trying to make happen that is frustrating for you. Pick one that you are finding so aggravating you don't know what to do next.

Describe the situation:

Now, unleash your topdog! What would you really like to do to respond to this situation? What is the wildest, most outrageous strategy you can come up with that would make this situation turn out right? Don't restrict yourself; don't worry about what should be. Work on the assumption that no matter what you come up with, everyone will approve of it.

Now, try to drag your underdog up into a sitting position. What is the safest, easiest, most low-risk, least-involved thing you can do to respond to the situation? You want to get in, do the barest minimum to respond to the situation, and then get out, preferably without being seen.

Finally, see if you can integrate the two extreme positions into a workable strategy. That is, take the creative, high-risk, fun elements of the topdog strategy and run them through a reality check from the underdog. What will emerge is a stronger, different strategy that will have a good potential for working.

The following is a simple example:

Topdog: Lock the kid in the basement, chained to the furnace, until his grades improve.

Underdog: Mention to the kid that he might try a little harder next period.

Integrated: Point out that his current grades are unacceptable and that people who maintain acceptable standards have more control over their own lives. Mention that he has one marking period in which to improve in order to maintain his current privileges. The choice is his.

Now try your version.

CHANGE-LEADER ACTIVITY:
DEALING WITH YOUR OWN RESISTANCE
Concept/Objectives

Working with resistance must be viewed as an integral and productive part of the change process, rather than as a painful and difficult chore to be avoided whenever possible. Before you can effectively work with others' resistance, it is essential that you honor your own. If you deny your own resistance, it is more difficult for you to understand and work with the resistance of group members, and it sets a norm for group members to avoid honoring and dealing with theirs.

Directions: In the space below, identify a change that you are presently working on (or one that you recently experienced) that you do not _personally_ support.

Change:

1. List all the reasons others have given you as to why you should support this change.

2. Summarize the reasons into a two-sentence case for making the change.

THE CHANGE LEADER

3. Now, <u>using complete sentences</u>, list all the reasons you have for resisting the change.

4. Again, summarize these reasons into a two- or three-sentence case for resisting the change.

5. Keeping your case for resistance in mind, can <u>you</u> now think of any reason that there might be some value in supporting the change?

CHANGE-LEADER ACTIVITY: RESISTING RESISTANCE
Concept/Objectives

People frequently disown their resistance in the very act of expressing it. Even though I know that I am resisting a proposed change—and am doing so aggressively—I refuse to take responsibility for it. The more that people take ownership of their own resistance, the easier it is to defend their positions or change them if they choose to do so in light of new information.

One way to get increased clarity and control over your own resistance is to verbally acknowledge it.

Directions: For each pair of statements below, mark the one that is most true of you when you find yourself in opposition to a demand for change from the organization. Even if neither one really represents you, choose the one with which you most closely identify. If you are doing this in a private place, it will help to read each choice out loud so that you can hear the options.

Proposed Change:

1. a. _____ I don't want to support the change.

   b. _____ I shouldn't support the change.

2. a. _____ I won't agree with a lot of the suggested changes.

   b. _____ I can't agree with a lot of the suggested changes.

3. a. _____ I choose to resist the organization's new direction.

   b. _____ I have to resist the organization's new direction.

4. a. _____ Mostly I dislike the change.

   b. _____ Mostly my group dislikes the change.

5. a. _____ The change is not in my best interest.

   b. _____ The change is not in the organization's best interest.

6. a. _____ I like to resist.

   b. _____ I feel obliged to resist.

7. a. _____ I don't see what's in it for me, if the change goes through.

   b. _____ I can't see what's in it for me, if the change goes through.

8. a. _____ I want to block the proposed change.

   b. _____ I need to block the proposed change.

9. a. _____ I don't see the benefit of this change for the organization.

   b. _____ I can't see the benefit of this change for the organization.

10. a. _____ This change won't work.

    b. _____ This change can't work.

SCORING KEY

Either choice on any question could be appropriate. In general, however, the more "a" responses you choose, the more you are owning your own resistance, which is positive. The more "b" responses you choose, the more you tend to blame your resistance on someone or something else.

If you chose:
10-9 "a" responses: You tend to take responsibility for your resistance and can work with it effectively.

8-6 "a" responses: You tend to avoid making the difficult decisions yourself.

5-0 "a" responses: You tend to see yourself as a victim of the organization, with little energy or courage to make things the way you would like them to be.

Option: _This instrument can be used to diagnose the nature of the group's resistance to the proposed change. Discussing how group members are resisting, before they address the change, could be beneficial. This is recommended only if the group is basically supportive and is highly growth oriented._

CHAPTER**SEVEN**

Negotiating Change

QUALITY AND ACCEPTABILITY

Any change is made up of two distinct elements: the quality of the change and the acceptability of the change (Maier, 1963). The quality of the change is the responsiveness of the change to the condition that needs to be improved. Quality is judged by whether the change accomplishes what was intended. The acceptability of the change refers to how readily the people who are involved in the change accept or support it. The effectiveness of any change process is based on these two elements.

If quality were the only concern, we might end up with a lot of objectively sound suggestions for changes that are totally unacceptable to the people who have to implement them. Their response would be disinterest, at the very best, and sabotage, at the very worst. On the other hand, if acceptability were the only concern, we might end up with a lot of complacent people who were unable to get the job done.

In the figure that follows, both the quality and the acceptability of particular changes are rated on scales of one to nine. The long-term effectiveness of a change can be illustrated by how much total area in the graph is covered. For example, a perfect change would be rated nine in quality and nine in acceptability, this would cover eighty-one "square units" of effectiveness.

In the two illustrations, change B has a much higher probability of producing good long-term results than does change A, even though the quality rating of change B is observably lower.

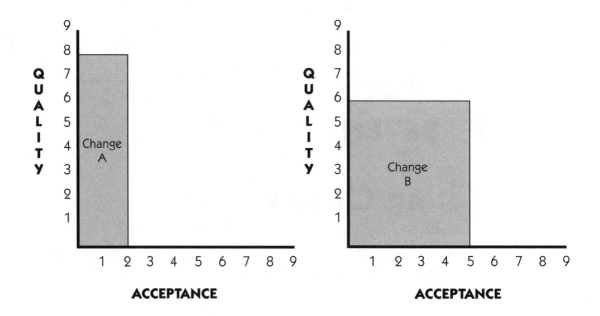

The Quality-Acceptance Relationship

The best strategy seems to be to first have a change that is responsive to the objective demands of the situation and then to be able to make it as acceptable as possible to the people who must implement it.

Any effort devoted to making a change more acceptable to those who are responsible for its implementation should be considered an investment! There are two reasons for this. First, this premise is consistent with the theme of this book which, if you will remember, states:

■ ■ ■

*No human being has the right to make a unilateral
decision that affects the lives of other individuals without
offering them a voice in that decision.*

■ ■ ■

Individual dignity and personal commitment are a direct function of having as much control over one's life as possible. We can refer to this as the principle of self-determination.

Second, taking the time to plan and work at the beginning of the change process with the people who will have to implement the change is a lot less expensive in terms of time, effort, and misery than dealing with a failed change attempt later on. As the saying goes, "pay now or pay later."

NEGOTIATING SKILLS

The more you can bring about a high-quality change through mutual negotiation, rather than by unilateral demand, the higher the probability the change will be acceptable to those who have to implement it. Therefore, one of the most important tools needed by a change leader is the ability to negotiate effectively. There are two aspects of negotiating effectiveness: *style,* which refers to each individual's unique approach to working with change, and *tactics,* which refers to specific dos and don'ts that will increase the probable acceptance of the change.

Negotiating Styles

How one approaches a negotiation is as individualistic a process as any other that requires creativity. Like all other human capacities, one's specific negotiating style can be viewed through the concept of polarities.

In looking at the figure that follows, at one end of the continuum is the tough battler. This type of negotiator's typical characteristics are aggressiveness, drive, and tenacity. At the very best, the tough battler is commanding, focused, and energized. At the very worst, the tough battler is impatient, overbearing, and stubborn. Winning is all that matters.

At the other end of the continuum is the supportive facilitator. This negotiation style is typified by being caring, sensitive to others, and conciliatory. At the very best, the supportive facilitator is open, helpful, and engaging. At the very worst, the supportive facilitator is saccharine, overly emotional, and submissive. Being nice to, and taking care of, people is all that matters.

Negotiating Style Continuum

As can be seen in the next figure, there is a third type of negotiator that is just as opposite from the supportive facilitator as from the tough battler. This is the cognitive reasoner. This negotiator is characterized as contemplative, rational, and analytical. At best, the cognitive reasoner is clear, methodical, and visionary. At worst, the cognitive reasoner is cold, obsessive, and petty. Being right is all that matters.

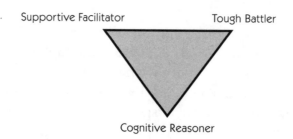

Supportive Facilitator   Tough Battler

Cognitive Reasoner

Negotiating Styles

If you look around you right now, there are probably hundreds of different colors, hues, and tints that you could differentiate, were you to take the time. Each color is made up of some combination of the three primary colors: red, blue, and yellow. In the same way, each individual's negotiating style is made up of some combination of the three basic negotiating styles.

Although each basic style has the potential to contribute to an effective individual negotiating style, no pure style can be effective by itself. A tough battler that isn't mediated, to some degree, by the other two types becomes a raging screamer. An unmodified supportive facilitator can quickly develop into a smothering helper. A cognitive reasoner that resists the influence of the other two styles readily turns into a cynical critic.

No specific style is any better than any other, just as no color is any better than any other. Each negotiating style has its own capacity for positively influencing a change process.

Although it is possible to have a negotiating style that is made up of equal parts of all three basic types, it is much more likely that your unique style will be characterized more by one basic type than another.

Styles that are dominated by either the tough battler or the logical reasoner share a common strategy. Both types are basically "topdog" negotiators, preferring to increase the driving forces toward change. The supportive facilitator, however, originates in the "underdog" and approaches the negotiation process by attempting to reduce the restraining forces that resist the change. Most people tend to identify more strongly with the two topdog types because they are more visible and forceful. In all probability, however, the more effective style in negotiating a long-term change is the "underdog" influence of the supportive facilitator.

Characterizing the Three Basic Styles

Although every identifiable negotiating style is as distinct and unique as the person who has it, there are some common tendencies associated with those that are dominated by the basic types. Being aware of these gives you some options for putting together negotiating teams. The more of a balance of the three styles you can bring to the negotiations, the higher the probability that you will be able to respond effectively to each new challenge of the negotiation, as it occurs.

The Tough Battler

Negotiators who are heavily influenced by the tough battler tend to be good at persuading, taking the lead, reducing ambiguity, taking risks, and reacting quickly to changes in negotiating conditions. If the tough battler were a bird, it would be an eagle.

On the other hand, tough battlers are not very good at weighing the pros and cons, calculating risks, responding to personal issues, analyzing data, waiting, and dealing with situations that require a great deal of sensitivity or empathy.

Their strength is in being persuasive, charismatic, assertive, self-confident, resilient, self-supportive, clear, and persistent. They function best in negotiations that require energy and perseverance. The payoff is in conquering the challenge.

The Supportive Facilitator

Negotiators who are strongly influenced by the supportive facilitator are good at contacting people, easing tension, small talk, helping all parties identify their needs, social interaction, finding common ground, generating optional solutions, and responding to personal or emotional problems. Were the supportive facilitator a bird, it would be a swan.

Supportive facilitators are not good at dealing with conflict head on, collecting or analyzing data, making clear demands, dealing with differences in status or rank, and functioning within tight time constraints.

Their strengths are that they are patient, good listeners, helpful, accepting, good at seeing peripheral issues, able to develop trusting relationships, and good at generating loyalty. They function best in working with people who are friendly and who are genuinely looking for a positive solution to the change problem. The payoff is in working with the interpersonal processes that lead to the best outcome with the greatest satisfaction.

The Cognitive Reasoner

The negotiators who are influenced most by the cognitive reasoner are good at analyzing problems, defusing emotional issues, concentrating on detail, technical problem solving, staying with the issue, and integrating variables. Were the cognitive reasoner a bird, it would be an owl.

Cognitive reasoners typically are not very good at responding to subjective elements or arguments, dealing with ambiguity, applying pressure, reacting quickly to changing situations, or dealing at the personal or emotional level.

Their strengths lie in being cautious, methodical, thorough, orderly, calming, analytical, precise, and credible. They function best when dealing with the objective and cognitive aspects of a change. The payoff is in beating the problem.

Dealing with Each of the Basic Styles

Once you have some understanding of your unique style (see the activity at the end of this chapter), it is a good idea to take the time to try to pinpoint the negotiating styles of the key people with whom you will negotiate the change. Knowing what attracts and what repels them can help you to maintain positive contact with them throughout the negotiation process. The following are a few basic "dos" and "don'ts" to keep in mind when dealing with various types of negotiators.

TOUGH BATTLER

DO	DON'T
1. Be brief, clear, and to the point.	1. Ramble on or overexplain.
2. Provide options for them to decide on.	2. Come up with ready-made solutions.
3. Focus on outcomes.	3. Disagree on a personal basis.
4. Persuade by referring to objectives.	4. Anticipate responses.
5. Ask questions.	5. Lecture.
6. Honor their resistance.	6. Withhold honest disagreement.
7. Make your points directly.	7. Overqualify or apologize for your position.

SUPPORTIVE FACILITATOR

DO:
1. Leave time for relating.
2. Show interest in them as people.
3. Find common positions.
4. Make demands in a nonthreatening manner.
5. Draw out their opinions.
6. Be patient.
7. Stress people-related benefits of the change.

DON'T:
1. Rush headlong into the negotiating process.
2. Manipulate or bully them.
3. Be cold or abrupt.
4. Leave things hanging.
5. Patronize them.
6. Push the change too strongly.
7. Attempt to decide for them.

COGNITIVE REASONER

DO:
1. Your homework.
2. Be direct and straightforward.
3. Support your ideas with data.
4. List pros and cons.
5. Be specific.
6. Maintain your objectivity.
7. When disagreeing, stay focused on the facts.

DON'T:
1. Be disorganized.
2. Use evidence from an unreliable source.
3. Rely on personal opinion as evidence.
4. Leave things vague.
5. Deal in generalities.
6. Be impatient.

The previous lists contain generalizations and are intended to assist you in maintaining your awareness. They are only part of the formula. When dealing with anyone, you must be aware of the specific differences that exist between you *at the moment* and respond to those.

Negotiating Tactics

Regardless of anyone's particular negotiating style, there are some things to keep in mind that will help you to maintain positive control when negotiating a change process. They are as follows:

1. Enter the negotiation process centered and clear.

2. Be able to describe the change in terms of a positive vision.

3. Avoid provoking others or being provoked.

4. Work *with* the resistance, theirs and yours.

5. Pay attention to shared goals.

6. Stay in control of the communication.

7. If possible, make an early, small concession.

8. When making a concession, ask for something in return, if appropriate.

9. Establish clarity at the outset about what elements are negotiable and what elements are not, on your side and on theirs.

Enter the Negotiation Process Centered and Clear

The clearer you are about what you want as an outcome for the change, the higher the probability that you will get it. If you are not clear, the people with whom you are negotiating will be even less so. As clarity decreases, you become more vulnerable because, in most cases, you will be outnumbered. As confusion increases, so does defensiveness, and the last thing you want is to have this turn into a win/lose or adversarial situation.

Frame the demand for change in the simplest, most specific, time-bounded, behavioral terms possible. It is also wise to have an idea of potential outcomes—costs and benefits that might result from the change.

Be Able To Describe the Change in Terms of a Positive Vision

One of the current criteria for leadership effectiveness at any level is the ability to create and communicate a vision. One aspect of communicating a vision is describing what is happening in the present, not only in terms of immediate outcomes but also in terms of the impact on future events.

Many—if not most—changes are intended to better an existing condition. In today's complex, interrelated systems, the change you are attempting to implement will impact future conditions as well. When initially presenting the change, a selling point is how the present change will have future positive impact and benefits for both the individual and the organization. Many changes that are unpopular because they have painful short-term effects may be shown to have very positive long-term benefits.

Avoid Provoking Others or Being Provoked

Most changes will evoke varying degrees of resistance, depending on what is being demanded and how much impact the implementers are permitted to have on the change. Rarely will the change evoke resistance to the point of open hostility.

In introducing any change, particularly unpopular change, the best strategy is to keep the process as impersonal as possible. Deal with the issues, not with the people. Always make sure that the change is being negotiated in specific, behavioral terms. The thing that must be avoided at all costs in negotiating change is personalizing the process.

Personalizing begins to occur the moment you stop dealing with the change and start dealing with the people whom you are trying to influence. This transition usually arises out of a sense of frustration and begins with statements such as "You just don't understand" or "I know why you're doing this...."

The opening shot can come from you or from the other side; the trick is to stop it the instant you are aware of what has happened. The moment the interaction leaves the behavioral level and moves to the discussion of others' attitudes, beliefs, motivations, or values, you are out of control. The almost inevitable result is that the emotionality of the interaction skyrockets, and mutual resistance escalates at nearly the same rate.

Work with the Resistance, Theirs and Yours

As was mentioned in the Introduction, a major feature of the Gestalt approach to change is the importance of resistance and how it is managed. Unless you are the sole creator of the change you are trying to negotiate, there is a strong probability that you may have some unidentified and/or unresolved resistance toward it yourself. This is normal. However, if you are going to be effective in managing others' resistance to the change, you will have to honor and be willing to work with your own resistance first.

There is a potential for benefits and drawbacks in every experience. For example, you can love everything about someone or something initially; after awhile, however, there are some things you begin to like better than others, and eventually there are some elements that you may not like at all. As long as the positives outweigh the negatives, you have a solid basis for a long-term relationship.

This progression is just as true for change as it is for relationships. The first and most important step is to give yourself permission not to like what you don't like about the change. If you can be accepting of what you don't like, the chances are that you will be accepting and less judgmental about what others don't like about the change. This creates some empathy on your part and will allow you to work with the change, and their resistance to it, in a more supportive and effective manner.

Identify Mutual Benefits

It is a safe assumption that most people, whether they'll admit it or not, are tuned in to WII-FM—What's in It for Me? Therefore, it is not a good idea to attempt to "sell" a change based on loyalty to the organization. On occasion, self-sacrifice and loyalty are situationally appropriate responses to what is going on. They are not a good basis, however, for conducting day-to-day interactions, and it's the worst tack to take in negotiating a change unless you are facing a real crisis.

It is sometimes easy to lose sight of the fact that in a majority of cases, what is good for the organization is also good for the individuals in it. This is a much better strategy to pursue when negotiating a change. Whenever possible, describe the change in terms of mutual benefits.

Stay in Control of the Communication

Negotiating techniques are effective only when supported by clear communications. As a change leader, you are in position to control the communication process. Following are a few tips for improving communications and avoiding personalizing the negotiations.

1. *Speak only for yourself.* Use "I" statements unless representing consensus opinion.

2. *If you want to know what another person is thinking, ask, don't hypothesize.*

3. *Don't ask a question if you want to make a statement.* "I think..." is much stronger and clearer than, "Don't you think that...?"

4. *State your disagreements clearly.* If others can't count on you to say "No" when you mean it, they won't believe you when you say "Yes" either.

5. *Avoid using words such as "only" or "just" when making a point.* They diminish the strength and impact of what you are saying.

6. *Don't say "Yes, but...."* It means "No."

7. *Talk to one person at a time.* Even when addressing the group, maintain eye contact with, and focus on, one person at a time. The others will hear you better.

8. *Deal with one issue at a time.* Keep the conversation focused. If a new topic arises, use group consensus to quickly choose one and postpone the other.

9. *When you have made your point, stop.* Less is more. The fewer the words and the shorter the words, the better.

10. *Don't Ask "Why?"* One of the quickest ways to lose control of the change process is to demand that people tell you why they want what they want. This makes you appear to be judging their motiva-

tion, and it personalizes the process. Make the assumption that everyone has the right to want what they want, including you. Deal only with *what* is wanted and the effects of that.

If Possible, Make an Early, Small Concession

In negotiation, both sides have to be perceived as being willing to consider reasonable options in regard to the issue. As change leader, you need to be seen as authentically supporting this perspective early in the negotiation process.

The quickest and surest means of effecting a change in another's response is to make a sudden and unexpected change in your own. Making a small, reasonable concession early on, particularly if you don't have to, establishes you as a reasonable person with whom others can negotiate. In addition, this will go along way toward establishing your credibility.

When Making a Concession, Ask for Something in Return, if Appropriate

This suggestion does not countermand the spirit of the preceding suggestion. Establishing yourself as a reasonable person who is willing to listen and respond does not imply that you are a dupe or a "soft touch."

You obviously will grant only concessions that are appropriate for you. This is the best time to ask for something back as the other side is a bit vulnerable, having just received something from you. This tactic also underscores the tough side of your negotiation style, which you want to keep focal. For example, you might say: "I am willing to take into account your concern about how much time this change in procedure will take, *if* I can count on you to give it your best effort while I am doing so."

Establish Clarity at the Outset About What Elements Are Negotiable and What Elements Are Not, on Your Side and on Theirs

Part of your credibility as a change leader and negotiator relies on your being seen as clear, credible, and supportive. The clearer you are about what is absolutely not negotiable about the change, the easier it will be to work with the elements that are, to some degree, negotiable. By being honest about this at the outset, you will be in a better position to choose the appropriate strategy for implementing the change.

With the best of intentions, some change leaders will soften the nonnegotiable elements or choose not to announce them, hoping that they won't come up. If the group becomes aware that this has occurred, you will lose your credibility, and your good intentions will count for nothing. If you promise something or imply that it might be available and it isn't, not only is your credibility gone, you may well increase the resistance to the change.

CONCLUSION

This chapter is not intended to provide a comprehensive discussion of the negotiation process. There are many programs and books dealing with the specific strategies and tactics of negotiation; I strongly recommend that you look into these.

What is important is that you understand the importance of having negotiating skills as part of your role as a change leader. Also, you need to understand how important individual style is, that you can negotiate effectively only from a style that fits you, and that you need to have a few tactics and strategies to approach the process with more confidence.

Reference

Maier, N.R.F. (1963). *Problem-solving discussions and conferences: Leadership methods and skills*. New York: McGraw-Hill.

CHANGE-LEADER ACTIVITY: NEGOTIATION-STYLE INVENTORY

Directions: Each item in this inventory contains an incomplete sentence followed by three different endings. Distribute ten points among the three endings to show how frequently each ending is characteristic of you. Use all ten points for each sentence.

1. In a dispute, my tendency is to:

___ do what's fair for everyone. ___ go for all I can get.
___ do what makes the most sense.

2. People who know me see me as a person who is:

___ trusting. ___ forceful. ___ orderly.

3. When people disagree with me, I tend to:

___ listen to their side. ___ argue my point. ___ respond with logic.

4. At my worst, I am apt to:

___ be passive. ___ go on the attack. ___ be stubborn in my opinions.

5. When buying something expensive, my tendency is to:

___ avoid the embarrassment of bargaining. ___ haggle over the price.
___ buy the item at the price that reflects its worth.

6. When I feel that I have been "taken" by a salesperson, my response afterward is to:

___ feel intimidated. ___ get really angry. ___ figure out where I went wrong.

7. When I am winning a hard-fought argument, I:

___ look out for the dignity of my opponent. ___ go for a complete and total victory.
___ feel vindicated in my superior logic.

8. When I make a request of someone in higher authority, and the answer is "No," I:

___ accept the "No." ___ become hostile. ___ find out what is available.

9. When someone in higher authority makes an unreasonable request of me, I tend to:

___ acquiesce. ___ resist. ___ point out the error of his/her judgment.

10. In a negotiation, at my best, I:

___ support people who are quiet. ___ provide the needed leadership.
___ keep the process emotionally defused.

SCORING KEY

<u>*Directions:*</u> Add the number of ratings from the first (left) column of choices and place the total number on line SF. Do the same for the second (middle) choices, and place the total number on line TB. Repeat for the third (right column) choices and place the total on line CR.

_____ SF　　_____ TB　　_____ CR

SF = Supportive Facilitator　　TB = Tough Battler　　CR = Cognitive Reasoner

CHANGE-LEADER ACTIVITY: NEGOTIATION ANALYSIS FORM

Concept/Objectives

The effectiveness of a change is based on its responsiveness to the situation and its acceptability to those who have to implement it. A first step in preparing to present a change is to analyze the change in terms of what is negotiable and what is nonnegotiable. If nothing is negotiable, tell the group members that at the beginning.

Directions: Analyze a proposed change by using the form that follows.

Proposed Change:

1. What is the objective of the change—what will improve in the environment as a result of the change?

2. What will implementing this change "cost," in terms of financial resources, employee resistance, lost opportunity, etc.?

3. What elements of the change are nonnegotiable?

4. What elements of the change are, to some degree, negotiable?

Looking at the "negotiable" list, for each item, state clearly and specifically what you *want*, then what you will *accept*, at the minimum. The difference between the two is what you have to negotiate.

Example:

Element: *Implementation time*

Want: *Three weeks*

Accept: *Five weeks*

Element: _____

Want: _____

Accept: _____

Element: _____

Want: _____

Accept: _____

Element: _____

Want: _____

Accept: _____

Element: _____

Want: _____

Accept: _____

Element: _____

Want: _____

Accept: _____

Element: _____

Want: _____

Accept: _____

Now rank the elements in terms of their impact on the entire change. The basic strategy is to negotiate from the least to the most important element.

Rank

1.

2.

3.

4.

5.

6.

CHANGE-LEADER ACTIVITY: NEGOTIATION PREPARATION

Concept/Objectives

If you enter a negotiation process assuming that the group will be responsive to the change, you could be right or you could end up with a painful surprise. If, on the other hand, you assume that the group is highly resistant to the change, the chances are you will create a self-fulfilling prophecy. Your wisest strategy is to test your assumptions as the negotiation process proceeds, modifying them as you go along. By assuming both possibilities, you will find it easier to stay centered and in touch with the group as the negotiation progresses.

Directions: Check out your assumptions about the proposed change by using the form below.

Proposed Change:

1. I personally support this change:

1	2	3	4	5	6	7
Not at all			Somewhat			Totally

2. The group supports this change:

1	2	3	4	5	6	7
Not at all			Somewhat			Totally

3. My boss supports this change:

1	2	3	4	5	6	7
Not at all			Somewhat			Totally

4. The persons in my group who are most likely to support me and/or the change are:

Because:

5. The persons in my group who are most likely to resist me and/or the change are:

Because:

6. Review your answers above, then respond to the three questions below.

What is the best outcome that could result from the negotiations?

What is the most catastrophic outcome that could result from the negotiations?

What do you think will really happen?

(Remember, these are *assumptions* to be tested. Stay loose!)

CHAPTER**EIGHT**

Situational Exclusion

There is an old saying that states: "It's an ill wind that blows nobody good." This means that no matter how bad something appears to be, it holds some potential good for someone. If this is true, then so is the opposite: No matter how good something appears to be, it potentially holds some ill for someone. This is particularly true in regard to the change process.

As I have discussed, the common myth is that those who want to make the change see the change as being good, and those who have to endure the change see it as being basically bad. The major strategy in response to this is to involve as many people as possible in the change process.

The myth is that the change will automatically be seen as bad. People don't resist change, they resist *pain*. Although there certainly are many changes that are justifiably resisted, there are also many changes that are welcomed by the work force. Such changes might be relaxation of dress codes or the opportunity for more control over one's work through structures such as self-directed work teams.

By stressing that change leaders need to be concerned about involving people, we set up a dilemma: "How do we foster employee involvement as an organizational value for supporting change and, at the same time, deal with the fact that sometimes employee involvement is situationally inappropriate?" To be more specific, "How do you exclude an employee for the good of the organization when the employee wants to be included in the change?"

CURATIVE AND PREVENTATIVE EXCLUSION

There are two forms of situational exclusion that the change leader must be aware of. The first is curative and the second is preventative. Although preventative exclusion is certainly the more preferred approach, curative exclusion is, by far, the easiest to implement.

Curative Exclusion

No matter how effective or supportive the change leader, occasionally there will be a situation in which either the change leader, an employee, or both will have overestimated the employee's ability to handle the change. What happens is that the employee and/or the change leader see only the benefits of the change and not the roadblocks. Formal programs in goal setting, job enrichment, and self-directed work teams periodically produce this type of overestimation. The error is also made by change leaders who want to see employees develop and therefore implement growth-related changes too quickly.

Once the employee and the change leader experience the failure of the change, it is a relatively easy thing to respond to the need to get the employee out of the stressful situation. So long as the change leader handles the situation supportively, the employee may even be appreciative of his or her removal from the stressful situation.

The curative approach is much simpler because the error has been made, a failure has occurred as a result of the error, and the change leader and the employee are both aware of all the contributing conditions. Because both are in agreement about what happened, the employee can be excluded from further participation in the change with minimal damage to his or her self-image. Although this specific attempt at including the employee has failed, both parties are to be congratulated. They attempted something new and risky and have had the opportunity to learn from it so that the next attempt will have a much higher chance of success.

Preventative Exclusion

To manipulate another old saying, "A pound of prevention is worth an ounce of cure." It is far more difficult to prevent inclusion errors than it is to cure them. However, prevention is the preferable approach in terms of what is in the best interests of the employee, the change leader, and the organization.

In preventative exclusion, the employee is excluded from taking part in the new change. Here, the change leader is saying, "I am not going to let you participate in this change, even though I may be letting others do it." There is no testing, no challenge, no risk. It is simply a matter of the change leader's judgment of the employee's ability.

By way of example, let me recount the incident that brought the issue of situational exclusion into focus for me. Some time ago, I had been consulting with a group of supervisors in a chemical plant. We had been working on problems that were challenging them, and Mike, the supervisor of shipping, came up with a real stumper. A very large special order had come in from a foreign customer. Because of the order's size and complexity, management had decided that this particular order would be processed strictly on overtime. The problem that Mike faced was that his most senior worker, Fred, didn't have the ability to process the complicated paperwork that this particular order required.

Not only was Fred to be denied the opportunity for more challenging work, he was to be singled out from his work group and denied the opportunity for overtime income. Mike had intentionally skipped the issue in the first round of overtime, but realized that confronting the issue could no longer be avoided. Just that morning he had informed Fred of the change in procedure and that he would not be included. Fred felt dejected, left out, and discriminated against. Mike felt guilty and somewhat helpless.

The most frustrating aspect of this problem was that nobody was at fault. It was not the employee's fault that he was not qualified to do more than his present job required. Nor was it the change leader's fault that a unique situation arose that called for a tough decision.

THE NATURE OF EXCLUSION

Under the best of conditions, exclusion is difficult. There is tremendous pressure in organizations today to honor diversity, and it is illegal in the U.S. (and considered immoral) to exclude people because of cultural differences. Exclusion is particularly painful and is usually experienced as rejection. There is probably nothing more damaging to the self-image than to be told, "You are not wanted here."

Most people would like to avoid hurting someone else, which makes exclusion a painful process for the excluder as well as for the person being excluded. This is doubly difficult when the exclusion occurs in the midst of trying to get everyone else involved.

There are two clear justifications for excluding someone from a change: one is lack of situational competence; the other is priority.

Exclusion Based on Lack of Situational Competence

To constructively exclude someone because of lack of situational competence, three conditions have to exist.

- The specific task or responsibility that the individual is to be excluded from must be something over and above the individual's present job duties and responsibilities.

- The change leader must communicate this clearly and must be very specific in explaining that the employee does not have the ability or the commitment to respond to the change at this time, and there must be evidence to support this decision.

- The exclusion must be only for this particular change. There is no implication that the exclusion will occur again under different circumstances. Whenever the individual is competent to respond to the change, he or she will be included.

An example covers all three conditions. In a change starting next week, technicians will respond to customer service calls without going through the sales rep whose account it is. Charlie, an excellent and very dependable technician, has very poor verbal skills and has been know to use profanity to express himself when frustrated—at times without even being aware of it. Obviously, the leader cannot let Charlie respond directly to customer service calls.

The change is outside Charlie's present job responsibilities. Charlie does not have the ability or willingness to immediately respond to the change. Charlie will be included in the change once he demonstrates the ability to communicate acceptably.

A second—and probably more common—example is situationally excluding a new employee from participation in a complex project because he or she is not familiar enough either with the company or with the technology required to perform satisfactorily.

When exclusion is dealt with under the three conditions, it provides several benefits to the individual and to the organization. These follow.

Appropriate Exclusion Prevents Failure Experiences

Being excluded, for whatever reason, is almost always painful. If dealt with respectfully, however, the pain can be temporary and basically nondamaging. If, on the other hand, appropriate exclusion is avoided, the resultant pain can be chronic and damaging. Allowing an employee to take on a task or responsibility that is destined for failure results in loss of self-confidence and ego damage for the employee, disappointment and strained working conditions for the change leader, a failure for the group, and damaged reputations all around.

Appropriate Exclusion Provides Needed Role Clarification

When a change leader excludes a group member from a specific change he or she, at the same time, is providing a clear boundary statement for that employee.

Telling a direct report, "I think that you can handle the new demands," lets the person know that he or she is ready for more responsibility and clarifies the areas of his or her contribution.

Telling the employee that he or she is not ready provides exactly the same function. Anything that the change leader does that results in individual group members becoming clearer about how they make their best contributions will result in better work, less confusion, and more stable working relationships.

In the example used previously, excluding Charlie from the change forces him to be aware of, and become responsible for, his present inability to handle customer contact professionally.

Appropriate Exclusion Provides an Impetus for Employee Development

When the situation requires that a specific group member be excluded from a specific job-related change, both the change leader and the employee become acutely aware of what the employee's limitations are. Rather than viewing the exclusion as a painful and humiliating encounter, the employee can be encouraged to regard it as an opportunity to become aware of his or her developmental needs and pursue them. At the same time, this affords the change leader the opportunity to become aware of how best to support the employee in his or her development through training, coaching, or other forms of organizational support. In the example used previously, getting Charlie enrolled in a verbal skills workshop might be an appropriate step.

Appropriate Exclusion Provides More Credible Change Leaders

The change leader who makes a point of involving everyone, all the time, as a matter of policy, is no more effective than the leader who excludes everyone from the change process as a matter of policy. The issue of inclusion or exclusion is not a matter of organizational dogma; it is a matter of ascertaining the existing conditions and then being able to respond appropriately.

The paradox here is that if the change leader is willing and able to exclude an employee when that is what is needed, it allows the change leader to better support the individual group member. For example, if I know that you, as the change leader, will exclude me when that is appropriate, I can more readily trust your judgment when you choose to include or involve me. When you are more confident in my ability to handle a challenging change than I am, your confidence is believable and solidly reinforces my own.

Exclusion Based on Priority

The second justification for excluding someone from a positive change is priority. This occurs when the employee's skills are equal to the demands of the change but are critically needed elsewhere; for example, if the employee is midway through a very important project or his or her talents are needed elsewhere. This is a matter of priority, not one of competence, but it still relates to the fact that the employee's best use of time is not on the new change project.

Excluding someone from doing something because of priority is easier to do because there is no attack on the employee's self-image. Unfortunately, the person will probably resent it even more. In excluding someone because of priority, you must be very clear that this is a one-time choice on your part and is not likely to happen again. If you have done your homework, the employee will understand the necessity of your decision, even though he or she may not like it. In this circumstance, you need to do something to make up for it as soon as you can. If you don't, you send a message that people who are doing important work well end up getting the less exciting opportunities, if any at all.

Although both competence and priority are important reasons for exclusion from a change effort, you will probably have do deal with the issue of competence more often. Therefore, the rest of this chapter will focus on that issue.

BLOCKS TO EXCLUSION

There are many conditions and signals from the environment that legislate against excluding people. Most of these are well-intentioned and generally productive. However, they should not be responded to without taking the uniqueness of each situation into account. Some of the blocks to exclusion are as follows:

Unwillingness To Hurt Others

This is an important and valid consideration. The change leader must consider whether *not* excluding the employee will result in much greater pain later on.

Unwillingness To Show a Lack of Confidence in the Employee

The concern is that if the change leader displays a lack of confidence in the employee's ability to handle the change, the employee's self-confidence will be eroded. Although there is a risk of this occurring, the change leader does not have confidence in the employee's ability to support the change, and the clearer the change leader is about this, the better.

The change leader can avoid damaging the employee's self-confidence by pointing out that the concern is centered on the change, and has no bearing on the employee personally or how he or she is performing his or her regular job.

Management Philosophy As Religion

Upper management will sometimes launch a change program with such force that the change leader fears being cast out as a heretic if he or she doesn't respond with total and unabashed enthusiasm. When this occurs, the fault is upper management's for not indicating where exceptions to the change may be appropriate. This is often compounded by the change leader's tendency to misinterpret management's desire for employee participation in the change as a managerial dictate to involve everybody all the time. Even if the change leader works for a manager who insists that everyone be involved regardless of circumstances, the change leader incurs much less risk by confronting the manager with a specific exclusion case than by colluding with the manager in setting up an employee for failure.

The Employee Doesn't Want To Play

No matter how good the change appears to be or how well-intentioned the change leader, not every employee is going to want to be involved. There is always the employee who is happy with the status quo and would prefer to be left alone. It is very easy to exclude someone who doesn't want to be involved. What is more difficult is having the change leader *not* see this as a personal failure.

For example, the change leader might say, "I'm sorry, Charlie, I'm not including you in the overtime project," and Charlie might reply, "Who cares?" The change leader then might think, "Why didn't he want to do this? I thought my involvement program was working; where did I go wrong?" The change leader may tend not to exclude Charlie the next time simply because Charlie would prefer to be excluded.

STRATEGY FOR EXCLUSION

Whether the situation calls for a curative approach or a preventative one, there is a six-step strategy that the change leader can use in meeting with the employee to make the exclusion more workable and easier on all concerned.

To make this strategy work effectively, two things need to be done. First, the change leader must do the necessary homework and must be able to show the employee demonstrable evidence that the employee is not ready to participate in the planned change. Second, the strategy is to be used as a guideline to help the change leader work through a difficult process, but it should not become a ritual to be followed step-by-step, regardless of the circumstances. Once the change leader is clear about the process and confident in his or her ability to work with the situation, the key is to put the strategy in the background and stay in touch with the employee throughout the meeting. The strategy follows.

1. Indicate That a Change Will Occur That Will Not Include the Employee

As soon as the employee has been greeted and seated, it is best to get right to the point. The employee needs to be told directly and clearly that a change is going to occur in which he or she will not be involved. The sooner the employee knows the situation, the better. If the change leader attempts to soften the blow by engaging in small talk or by being defensive or apologetic, the situation is likely to become difficult to control.

In addition, it is essential that the change leader take full responsibility for the decision to exclude the employee and not try to spread the blame to the situation, the boss, or the organization. By saying something like, "Charlie, I have decided not to include you on the customer-service project," the change leader reinforces his or her role as leader and sets the stage for clearer communication in the rest of the meeting.

2. Explain the Reasons for the Exclusion in a Friendly and Supportive Manner

It is essential that the change leader's choice to exclude the employee be supported by clear, behavioral evidence. This is one of the few times in organizational life in which the leader is fully accountable to the employee. The employee has every right to know the reasons the change leader has for excluding him or her.

The change leader must be clear about the additional skills that the planned change requires and then must be just as clear in pointing out that the employee does not have these qualifications at this time. By being able to present evidence that the employee does not have the requisite skills to successfully participate in the change at this time, the change leader sets the stage for a more productive meeting in two ways.

First, the situation is *depersonalized*. Issues of personality, attitudes, and working relationships are no longer relevant. The focus is on the change requirements and conditions. This allows the employee to realize that there is no personal fault involved and, therefore, the risk of ego damage to the employee is greatly reduced. The second advantage to having all the data available is that once the situation is made clear to the employee, the change leader can shift roles from "excluder" to "supporter."

3. Listen and Respond Empathically

A distinction needs to be made between the word "sympathy" and the word "empathy." Sympathy connotes an *emotional* link between two people. The implication of sympathy is "I feel what you feel" or "I feel badly for you." Sympathy occasionally can be appropriate when pain—whether physical or psychological—is so intense that the person is having difficulty in supporting himself or herself. In general, however, sympathy should be avoided in business relationships.

Empathy, on the other hand, connotes an *understanding* between two people. The implication of empathy is that "I understand what you feel." Empathy is vital in maintaining good contacts and supportive relationships among people. The function of empathy is to let the person in pain know that what he or she is experiencing is understood and is legitimate. This promotes self-support, rather than external support.

When an employee has been informed that he or she is to be excluded from a change and why the decision was made, the response is not likely to be positive. The range of responses is virtually limitless, from apathy to dejection, from anger to self-recrimination.

It's at this stage that the change leader really gets control of the process. This is done by *listening* to what the employee is saying (or not saying) and responding empathically.

Just as it would be inappropriate for the change leader to criticize the employee for feeling sad, it is just as inappropriate for the change leader to attempt to talk the employee out of what he or she is feeling. Statements such as, "You shouldn't feel that way," "Its not so bad," and "Things will look better tomorrow" only prolong the bad feelings and convince the employee that the change leader wasn't listening and doesn't really care.

If the employee responds with anger or in a hostile manner, it is wise for the change leader to realize that the hostility is *defensive*. The employee is in the act of protecting himself or herself, not attacking the leader. In most cases, all the change leader has to do to maintain control and a safe environment is to listen and then respond with something like, "I can understand why you are angry with me right now, given the decision I have made."

By encouraging the employee to express any negative feelings, the change leader can help the person to honor and dispose of those feelings in the shortest amount of time.

An additional aspect of this process is that by encouraging the employee to openly state feelings about being excluded, the change leader can hear what is really bothering the employee. The individual's primary concern may be loss of income, humiliation, denied opportunity for growth and advancement, feelings of being inadequate, or something else. By discovering the specific elements that are of concern to the employee, the change leader may be in a position, later on in the meeting, to do something of a positive and substantial nature about them.

4. Recognize the Employee's Specific Contributions and Performance on the Job

Once any negative feelings have been stated and acknowledged, the change leader can offer support to the employee. This is done by emphasizing that the decision to exclude the employee from the change is no reflection on the employee's performance on the job or other day-to-day contributions.

It is essential that the change leader be able to cite specific instances of the employee's on-the-job effectiveness, the times when they occurred, and what the effects were, whenever possible. If the change leader fails to be specific, the attempt to bolster the employee's self-image will be perceived as an insincere human-relations ploy. This is guaranteed to make the situation worse, rather than better.

5. Identify and Support Actions That Will Improve the Employee's Ability

Remember that the employee has been excluded from the change because of a lack of specific capability, whether it be technical or interpersonal. When the employee's peers are being included in the change, the chances are that the individual does have the *potential* to participate in the change. The change leader can use the exclusion as an opportunity to begin to develop this potential.

One of the major tenets of human resource development is that most people can be developed to greater competence and responsibility. If the change is more than the worker can handle, and it's just dumped in his or her lap, the inevitable result is failure and an erosion of self-confidence.

If things have gone well in the preceding four steps of the strategy, the meeting can take a more positive direction. For example, if the situation were one of excluding Charlie from responding directly to customer service requests because of his poor verbal skills, the change leader can now help Charlie do something about this, if he so desires. Once Charlie sees that it is his lack of a needed skill, rather than the change leader's whim, that caused the exclusion, he may be willing to make some changes that could help.

An even better illustration might be in regard to a lack of technical competence. Assume that you are the change leader. In your opinion, the employee does not have the skills necessary to implement a change. The following steps can be taken to use exclusion as a basis for the employee's development.

1. You must tell the employee, *specifically,* what essential skills are presently lacking and/or what evidence is available that contributed to the decision to exclude.

2. You must help the employee to see the problem from your perspective and you must get a reasonable amount of objective concurrence from the employee. If this is not possible, there needs to be an open and frank discussion. Maybe you have not made the right decision.

3. When you obtain concurrence, work jointly with the employee on a plan of development for the employee to pursue. For instance, you might set up a mentoring relationship between the employee and a more experienced peer. A second choice is to include the employee in the change, but only in the less challenging aspects, under some direct supervision. Another option is to provide some on-the-job-training for the employee. A fourth choice is to have the employee enroll in off-site training to improve his or her skills in the targeted area. Any one or a combination of these steps would turn a situation of personal rejection into one of growth and opportunity.

4. Establish an action plan and a timetable, with checkpoints included, to monitor the employee's progress.

5. Work with the employee to establish an objective measure of competence to indicate when the employee has mastered the required skill.

6. When step 5 has been successfully concluded, acknowledge the employee as available for inclusion in the change project.

The most important aspect of using this process to deal with exclusion issues is that it encourages the employee to take the responsibility and do something positive to change his or her work life, other than complaining about how unfair it is.

A second consideration in this step is equity. No matter how clear and demonstrable the reasons for excluding the employee, he or she is still likely to feel that he or she has been dealt with unfairly, to some degree. To some degree this is probably true. Under these circumstances, there is nothing wrong with doing something that restores some semblance of equity, so long as it does not compromise the organization or you as the change leader. For example, if the employee is primarily concerned about the loss of income that the exclusion represents, you might offer him or her the next opportunity to work overtime, if it does not exceed his or her competence.

6. End the Meeting on a Positive Note

Just as it is important how the meeting begins, it is important how it ends. The employee should leave the meeting feeling as good about himself or herself as the situation allows. The closing step of the strategy is ending the meeting by summarizing the constructive and positive aspects of the situation.

Depending on what action steps have been agreed on, this is an excellent opportunity for the change leader to express confidence in the employee's ability to succeed in the planned actions. It is appropriate for the change leader to express specific appreciation for the employee's cooperativeness during the meeting and appreciation for the work he or she is doing.

This strategy was collaboratively developed with myself, Mike, and the other supervisors who were mentioned earlier. It was done in response to Mike's request for help in handling the exclusion of Fred, his most senior worker, from the special overtime project. The strategy was implemented successfully, as follows:

1. Mike asked Fred to come into his office. Mike briefly explained the nature of the project and stated his concern that Fred would not be able to handle the complex paperwork that was part of the project.

2. Mike showed the paperwork to Fred, explained what would be required, and quickly got Fred's concurrence that this was something that Fred did not want to tackle at the time.

3. Fred, although understanding the reasons, still felt bad about being excluded from the project. He felt inadequate because he was not up to the job. Mike listened patiently to what Fred was saying and acknowledged that he understood how this was painful for Fred.

4. Mike then reassured Fred that he was pleased with Fred's work on the job and cited some specific examples.

5. Mike asked Fred if he would like to do something to improve his ability to process paperwork, so that he could be included should a project like this happen again. Fred declined the offer but said he would like to think about it.

6. Mike thanked Fred for his understanding and assured him that he would be first in line for the next regular overtime project.

CONCLUSION

The key to a successful exclusion meeting is to approach it as an unpleasant but necessary part of the change leader's function. The meeting can be—and should be—a problem-solving session, rather than a punishing or humiliating experience.

There are several things that the change leader should be aware of in order to keep the meeting positive. First, do not use the meeting for any corrective purpose other than to deal with the exclusion issue. Ending the meeting with something like, "Before you go, let me ask why you were an hour late this morning" is sure to destroy any gains you may have made up to this point.

On the other hand, it is fine to move the subject to a new area, once the exclusion issue is finished, e.g., by saying something like, "Charlie, as long as you are here, I'd like to get your opinions of the Digby project." This shift in focus emphasizes that the exclusion issue is finished and allows the employee to move back onto familiar ground where he or she is coming from a position of strength. Obviously, you should not attempt to manipulate the situation so that this occurs, but if something is available, go ahead and use it.

A second caution is to not rush the process. In most cases, the exclusion meeting will be short and to the point. There is no way, however, to accurately gauge how any employee will react. What could be a minor annoyance for one person could be major disaster for another. The objective is to conduct the meeting well, not necessarily quickly. Depending on the magnitude of the exclusion and the emotional state of the employee, it might take two meetings to resolve the issue. Regardless of conditions, give it the time it takes to get it completely resolved. Remember, slower is faster.

CHANGE-LEADER ACTIVITY: PERSONAL BLOCKS TO EXCLUSION

Concept/Objectives

Excluding people is a very painful and awkward process, particularly in view of the current practice of including as many people as possible. When exclusion is appropriate, it is necessary to be able to do it effectively. One way to begin is to surface and honor your own resistance to exclusion.

Directions: Respond to the questions below as honestly as you can. Although each situation is different, try to make a general statement about how you feel.

1. Excluding people bothers me:

1	2	3	4	5	6	7
Not at all			Somewhat			A lot

2. Being excluded by others bothers me:

1	2	3	4	5	6	7
Not at all			Somewhat			A lot

3. I believe that regardless of the reason, excluding someone makes them feel bad and should be avoided at all costs.

1	2	3	4	5	6	7
Not at all			Somewhat			A lot

4. I believe that excluding someone from a specific activity destroys group cohesion.

1	2	3	4	5	6	7
Not at all			Somewhat			A lot

5. I think that everyone on a team prefers to be included in all group decisions and activities.

1	2	3	4	5	6	7
Not at all			Somewhat			A lot

6. Regardless of opinion to the contrary, I believe that the participative-leadership style is the most effective for group and team activities.

1	2	3	4	5	6	7
Not at all			Somewhat			A lot

7. I believe that consensus decision making is the most effective.

1	2	3	4	5	6	7
Not at all			Somewhat			A lot

8. It is important that group and team members spend time together outside the work setting.

1	2	3	4	5	6	7
Not at all			Somewhat			A lot

9. Team members should be encouraged to attend organizational social functions.

1	2	3	4	5	6	7
Not at all			Somewhat			A lot

10. It is more important for group members to be aware of how they are similar and what they have in common than it is for them to be aware of their differences.

1	2	3	4	5	6	7
Not at all			Somewhat			A lot

SCORING KEY

0-15: You have no problems with excluding others and probably need to be sure that you are not doing it inappropriately.

16-30: You believe that excluding others is an acceptable alternative, although one needs to be careful about how it is done so as to minimize pain.

31-45: If the situation calls for it, you can exclude others, although not without considerable feelings of guilt on your part.

46-60: Exclusion is only acceptable for you in the most critical situations—and then just barely. You will do almost anything to avoid it, including risking the group's effectiveness.

60+: You will never exclude anyone, regardless of the circumstances.

CHANGE-LEADER ACTIVITY: HONORING YOUR GUILT

Concept/Objectives

Despite a lot of popular opinion to the contrary, feeling guilty serves a vital function in maintaining effective work and interpersonal relationships *if* you are actually guilty of doing something wrong or destructive. Feeling guilt—or conscience—is critical in stopping us from doing things that are destructive or hurtful to others.

The problem in dealing with guilt is that sometimes others would like us to feel guilty when we have done nothing wrong. In most cases, this arises out of our failure to meet their <u>unstated</u> expectations for us, and they are disappointed. They now want us to take full responsibility for their feelings and to feel terrible for having not lived up to their expectations.

There is a Gestalt axiom to keep in mind in dealing with your own guilt: "You are only—and totally—responsible for your own actions. You are <u>never</u> responsible for someone else's feelings." If you are feeling guilty and want to do something about it, try the following activity.

Directions:

1. Briefly describe the situation about which you feel guilty.

> Example:
>
> Situation: *"I excluded Charlie from the current overtime project."*

2. In retrospect, was this an appropriate response?

Yes _____ No _____

If your response is "yes," proceed immediately to the next activity, "Reducing Your Guilt." If your response is "no," proceed with this activity.

3. What did you do that was inappropriate, wrong, or hurtful?

4. Make a final judgment of yourself.

Guilty _____ Not Guilty _____

If you judge yourself "not guilty," walk away from this; it is over. If you judge yourself "guilty," proceed to step 5.

5. If you find yourself guilty, follow the procedure below:

   a. Approach the other person and admit your guilt.

   b. Apologize and explain what happened.

   c. Negotiate a sentence for you to serve. (In many cases, the admission and apology will be all the "sentence" required. In other instances, some type of action will be required to obtain closure on the issue for both of you.)

   d. After the mutually agreed-on sentence has been served, _let go_.

   e. On occasion, the other person will refuse to talk to you about the issue or ill make an outrageous and unacceptable demand for equity. If the other person persists in this way after your _second_ attempt to atone, forget it! You have met your obligation, and the other person is free to feel as "sinned against" as he or she chooses. This is his or her choice and is no longer your problem!

CHANGE-LEADER ACTIVITY: REDUCING YOUR GUILT

Concept/Objectives

Guilt, _when not based in fact_, almost always produces resentment. In dealing with such guilt, you have two choices. The first choice is to suffer with the guilt, whether it be self-inflicted or other-induced. The second choice is to disown it as not being yours. This is a relatively simple process that can be accomplished by following the steps described below.

Directions:

1. Describe the exclusion: who was involved and why it happened.

2. In the spaces below, complete as many statements as you can that begin with the words, "I feel guilty because _____"

Example:

I feel guilty because _Charlie won't get to participate._

I feel guilty because _____

I feel guilty because _____

I feel guilty because _____

I feel guilty because _____

I feel guilty because _____

3. Convert each of the "I feel guilty" statements to a statement directed toward the other person that begins with the words, "I resent you because...."

> Example:
>
> I resent you because *I now have to find someone else to do your work on the project.*

I resent you because _____

I resent you because _____

I resent you because _____

I resent you because _____

I resent you because _____

4. Picture the other person sitting in an empty chair in front of you. Get a good image of the person. Now, in your mind, "maintaining eye contact" and in a strong voice, read the list of resentment statements to the other person. Begin each statement with his or her name. When you have completed this activity, check to see how much, if any, guilt is left.

CHANGE-LEADER ACTIVITY: EXCLUSION EXERCISE

Directions: Four scenarios are described below. In each case:

1. Determine if you would or would not exclude the person from the change activity.

2. Explain your thinking in regard to the choice.

3. State what you would do and how you would inform the person if exclusion were your choice.

There are no preferred answers. The challenge is to determine what _you_ would do.

Scenario 1

You are leading your organization's United Way campaign this year. The most difficult part of this job is to get fellow employees to volunteer their time. Ella is a new employee who, although extremely enthusiastic, has not proven to be very reliable. She fully embraces each assignment, but often leaves parts incomplete or unchecked. She has just burst into your office volunteering to help in this year's United Way campaign.

___ Include   ___ Exclude   ___ Other

Your reasoning:

You would do:

Scenario 2

You are the supervisor of a production crew. As part of its commitment to community service and development, your company has hired a number of intellectually challenged people for some of the entry-level positions. Alex is one such person in your crew. He is industrious, very likeable, and quite dependable. You and the other crew members genuinely appreciate him as a fellow worker and person.

You have just been informed that a new process is being introduced that will change the current technology appreciably. Your entire crew has been scheduled to undergo three days of intense training in the new process.

___ Include   ___ Exclude   ___ Other

Your reasoning:

You would do:

Scenario 3

You are the supervisor of a design group in a small, but very successful, privately owned company. The owner is a progressive manager who is a joy to work for, with one glaring blind spot. His son, who is not very talented, makes up for it by being fairly arrogant. A new and critical project has just been assigned to your team. The boss's son has just approached you demanding to be included in the project.

___ Include   ___ Exclude   ___ Other

Your reasoning:

You would do:

Scenario 4

Your production team has just been informed that it has been selected to share responsibility with the design team for the creation and presentation of a new prototype. This means that both groups have to act in concert and must work very closely together if the project is to be a success.

You happen to know that Sally, one of your most creative and hard-working group members, has a very bad personal history with Carl, the supervisor of the design team. As a matter of fact, Carl has been overheard saying that there is no way he is going to work with Sally.

___ Include   ___ Exclude   ___ Other

Your reasoning:

You would do:

CHAPTER**NINE**

Implementing Change

Some time and effort will have to be invested in planning a change if it is going to be effective and implemented easily and accurately. Most of the problems that arise out of change processes are the result of one of two conditions. Either not enough thought was given to the change's implementation or there was insufficient consideration of the resistance that frequently accompanies change.

As with most things, it is far less costly in terms of time spent and risk taken to take the time to plan the change before beginning it. The following considerations will help you to implement change strategies more effectively.

SOME FACTS ABOUT CHANGE

The Law of Distance

■ ■ ■

The farther the demand for change is from the point of implementation, the greater the resistance to the change.

■ ■ ■

The ways in which people regard authority are as varied as any other individual responses. However, the law of distance suggests that, in general, the more distant the source of the change, the more people are going to resist it. This observation is a spinoff of the law of self-determination, in that the farther the demander for change is from those who have to implement it, the less input and involvement people will have in making the change happen.

The fact that someone in higher authority thinks that the change is a good idea does not mean that the employees are going to support it automatically. It is likely that the opposite will occur. This is something to keep in mind as you select your strategy.

The Law of Complexity

■ ■ ■

The more complex the change, the greater the need to introduce it slowly.

■ ■ ■

Whenever a change is introduced, there is a decrease in initial performance. This is natural and to be expected. Whenever a change is introduced, there is a disruption in the work process. The employees must go through a process of learning something new or getting used to a new condition. Time must be allowed for the change to become familiar and natural.

It is the change leader's role to both support the change and to manage the temporary decrease in performance that frequently accompanies it.

One of the paradoxes of implementing change is that "slower is faster." The more time you spend in planning the change and implementing it correctly, the less time you are going to have to spend in apologizing, revising, and attempting it again.

The Change Leader Must Negotiate Reasonable Expectations for the Change Effects

Regardless of the intent, if the change being initiated overtaxes the employees' present capabilities or challenges their existing value systems, failure is likely.

The more you can involve the employees in the change process, the higher the probability that failure can be avoided. If resistance can be reduced to a reasonable level and there is a reasonable level of trust, the employees will tell you what they are capable of. The last thing you need is for the employees to agree to something and then forget about it.

Changes Often Provide the Opportunity for Training

There are many side benefits of a successful change project, not the least of which is the increased competence of employees.

As change leader, you can use almost any change project to develop some kind of training opportunity for your employees. Not only will this ensure a higher probability that the change effort will be successful and resisted less, it also will meet the ongoing need for employee growth and development.

Organizational Support Must Be Provided Throughout the Change Process

Your responsibility as the change leader goes beyond implementing the change in the system. For a change to be adopted quickly and effectively, it frequently requires the change leader to elicit the active support of upper management, staff, and outside sources, particularly if the change originated in any of these.

Too Enthusiastic a Response to a Change Can Be As Problematic As Too Much Resistance

Sometimes the change represents a positive impact on the group and generates a large amount of enthusiasm. The result of this is that employees may overestimate their capabilities and attempt to set performance or behavioral standards that are too high. You need to point out that challenging, but real, expectations are what make changes effective.

The Change Leader Doesn't Have To Like the Change

In resisting a change, employees might demand to know what you think about the change. Their motivation is to have you agree with them that the change is ill-conceived or unreasonable.

Although an effective change leader should never do anything that will subvert the implementation of the change, at some time, he or she may not be able to personally support a specific change, particularly if he or she is in full agreement with the employees. One thing the change leader can do is to say something like the following: "Whether I personally agree with the change or not is of no importance. What is important is that the change has to be implemented. We don't have to 'like it' to do our job of implementing it."

THE FOUR CHANGE CONDITIONS

	Externally Imposed	Internally Imposed
Negotiable	C1	C2
Nonnegotiable	C3	C4

The Four Change Conditions

C1: External and Negotiable

This type of change is the most common. It occurs when a source outside the work group imposes a change or condition on the group and allows the group some latitude in the implementation of the change. Examples of this type of change are broad policy shifts and organizational value statements or goal statements. The key factor is that the change is presented in terms of conditions or results, but the actions are left, in whole or in part, to the implementing group.

C2: Internal and Negotiable

This variety of change occurs when the change creators and implementors are the same. Examples are: changes in work design, changes in responsibilities, changes in group norms, group-generated goals or objectives, and any change made by a self-directed work team. The key factor is that the group is initiating and implementing the change.

C3: External and Nonnegotiable

This type of change comes from the outside and is as demanding in regard to the implementation process as it is in regard to the outcome. There is no room for variance. Examples include new safety regulations, legal statutes, and pricing schedules. The key factor is that the implementors must comply with the change as put forth or suffer the consequences for noncompliance.

C4: Internal and Nonnegotiable

This type of change is rare but does occur. It can be related to internal norms and values of the group or it can be in response to something physical. It frequently is initiated through a quick, unanimous consent and in response to a clear, unanticipated, and unacceptable condition. Examples are: a response to a safety risk (e.g., "from now on we can't shortcut through level 7") or a response to illegal or unacceptable behaviors. The key factor is that the group sees an immediate threat to itself or its members and responds strongly to it.

CHOOSING THE RIGHT STRATEGY

Change condition C1 is the most common; C3 is the next most common; C2 occurs occasionally; and C4 occurs rarely. It is helpful to be aware of them all so that you can respond confidently to each change situation as it arises.

In this chapter, the strategy for C1 is called S1; the strategy for C2 is S2, and so on. As C1 is the most common type of change, we will go into detail in explaining the strategy (S1) to be used with it. The strategies for the other conditions will be presented as variations of S1.

S1: External and Negotiable

Describe the Change in Detail

The group members' initial contact with the proposed change should be as positive as the situation allows. The first impression is the most lasting. If you initiate a change by saying, "I know you aren't going to like this but...," you can rest assured that is exactly what the outcome will be.

It is very important that the change be described in as clear, concise, and positive terms as possible. In describing the change, be as specific as you can: what the change is, why the change is occurring, whom the change will affect (in terms of outcomes and implementation), when the change will take place, and how the change will be implemented.

Explain the Benefits.

Be Clear About the Advantages of the Change. Although concern for others and altruism are laudable characteristics, most sustained change will emerge from a condition of enlightened self-interest. That is, most people are tuned in to WII-FM—What's in It for Me. This is natural, and there is nothing wrong with it. The more you can describe the change in terms of benefits, the higher the probability that the change will be accepted and implemented. Following are examples of how changes can be described in terms of benefits.

CHANGE	BENEFIT
Automation	Better sanitation, more potential profit
Relocation	Less rush-hour traffic, closer access to distribution centers
Schedules	Better work hours, more available to telephone customers
Job Design	More challenge and control, more efficiency
Overtime	More income for workers and company
New Boss	Clean slate, opportunity to look at processes

Examples of Changes and Benefits

Benefits should be described as early as possible when introducing a change, because people tend to take a reflexive, negative stance as soon as they hear the word "change." If the change leader introduces the good side of the change, there is less chance that random fear will emerge.

Explain What Has Not Changed. It is important for everyone to understand that change does not necessarily threaten the current state of stability. Planned change does not imply chaos; it can be even more stabilizing than the current situation because the change is in response to new conditions. Just because a change occurs in one aspect of the employees' work life, there is no implication that other things are going to change as a result. For example, you may have a new schedule, but the organization's goals, standards, resources, and interpersonal relationships have not been altered.

Point Out the Costs for Not Making the Change. Planned change occurs with the objective of making something better. One way the change leader can facilitate the change is to make sure that the employees understand what could happen if the change did not occur. For example, not paying overtime now means less chance of layoffs next month.

Listen to Reactions

Any change is probably going to produce some negative reaction, regardless of what that change might be. This is natural and healthy, and something is wrong if you don't get some resistance.

Working with the resistance supports the change effort. A critical skill at this stage is the ability to really listen to the employees' concerns and be supportive of them.

Get the Group's Involvement

The more negotiable the elements of the change, the higher the probability that you can get employee involvement. It is essential that you be honest about what is and what is not negotiable in the change. This will not only set clear guidelines for appropriate action, it will heighten your credibility.

The specific techniques for getting active individual and group involvement in the change process are covered in Chapter 5.

As you honor and respond to resistance, you can begin to redefine the change in terms of those elements that are negotiable and those that are nonnegotiable. Then if the group is large it can be divided into subgroups. The groups then engage in problem solving about how best to implement the change.

Get Agreement on an Action Plan

Once the group has decided how best to implement the change, a specific action plan needs to be developed. This should specify the following:

- exactly what is to be done (each action step),
- by whom each action is to be done, and
- when each action is to be completed.

It is usually the change leader's responsibility to identify and contact any external supports and resources needed to help the implementation. The change leader also oversees and supports the change itself.

Thank the Group Members for Their Cooperation

Change is always difficult; thanking the employees for their openness and their cooperation is very important. In addition, it allows you to establish a feedback process in encouraging the employees to come to you if there are any problems with the implementation, any suggestions for better ways to implement the change, or any need to discuss new concerns or resistances that arise from the implementation.

S2: Internal and Negotiable

Describe and Get Agreement on the Conditions That Are Suggesting/Demanding Change

Internal and negotiable change will generate the least resistance because it is initiated by the implementing group and emerges from a perceived need to make something better. It is important that all group members have an opportunity to identify the existing condition and comment on whether or not it needs to be changed. It is likely that not everyone will initially agree on the condition or whether it requires a change. When there is consensus that some change would be desirable and that there is a range of options, it is time to proceed to the next step.

Get Consensus on the Causes of the Present Condition

As has been noted before, there are two problems that tend to make the implementation of change difficult. The first is not acknowledging and working with the resistance; the second is implementing the change too quickly.

Once a problem or condition has been identified, there is a strong tendency to look immediately for a solution and then accept and implement the first one that looks like it has some potential. This is usually done without even looking for the cause of the problem! This is a good time to remember the axiom, "slower is faster."

Previously discussed techniques such as force-field analysis and cause-and-effect analysis are extremely useful for getting at the causes of the problem or condition that needs to be changed. Your most difficult job in managing the process at this point is in getting the group to identify the cause(s) of the problem *before* any move is made to come up with a solution (change) to respond to it.

Actively Involve the Group in Developing a Change That Will Correct the Condition

Using either free wheeling brainstorming or the nominal group technique, the group now generates a list of possible solutions that would respond to the primary cause(s) of the problem. The list is prioritized by triage, and one solution is selected by consensus.

Agree on an Action Plan To Implement the Change

Once the group has formulated a response to the change, an action plan needs to be developed for the implementation. This plan should specify what actions are to be taken, who will take each action, and when each action will be completed.

Identify External Resources and Impacts

It is highly likely that any change that a group initiates will have some ripple effect outside the work group itself. Once the actions necessary to implement the change have been identified and agreed on, it is very important that areas of potential impact *and* sources of support are clearly identified and contacted. It is the change leader's responsibility to identify and contact any external resources or support needed to make the implementation happen, along with any other parts of the organization whose work life might be affected by the internal change.

Devise and Install a Feedback Process To Monitor the Implementation of the Change

This last step is extremely important for the long-term success of the change. It is important to establish a feedback process to monitor the effects of the change, because new situations may arise that could distract energy away from the change process. In addition, because it is the work group itself that initiated and is implementing the change, there may be no other monitoring source available.

S3: External and Nonnegotiable

Describe the Change and Explain Why It Is Being Implemented

External and nonnegotiable change is the easiest to implement but it is the most difficult in terms of working with the resistance.

The change needs to be described to the employees as quickly and as clearly as possible. As the employees will have no input into how the change will be implemented, it is important that the need for the change be conveyed at this time. Even if the employees do not like the change, they can at least understand why management has made the particular decision.

Explain Specifically Who Is To Do What

One way to make the change process as quick and painless as possible is to plan it ahead of time. Make every effort to remove as much complexity as you can. This includes explaining who is to do what. For example, "Starting the first of next month, the 'A' operator on each shift will be responsible for completing the shift's status report and filing it." The more "matter of fact" you make the change and its implementation sound, the higher the possibility they will be taken that way.

Ask for Questions or Problems

External and nonnegotiable change, regardless of its content, will be resented and resisted because the employees have no input in something that will affect their work lives. You can minimize the negative effects by encouraging open expression of all the feelings about the change, including resentment and resistance. It is important that you give all employees an opportunity to state what they do not like about the change.

Because you will be working with some resistance, fight the temptation to speed up the process. Although you do not want to drag it out a moment longer than necessary, you do want to give all employees the opportunity to have their say and be done with it.

Honor the Resistance

By acknowledging uncertainty and negative feelings as authentic and understandable reactions to something new, you may be able to minimize negative effects of the change.

Clearly Define the Possibilities

Sometimes there may be some leeway in providing support or assistance to the employees in initiating the change, and every opportunity should be taken to explore this and manage it. While you are exploring the possibilities, do not hint or promise that something will happen.

Above all else, you must never imply that there is any chance of the change being modified if there really is none. You are much better off stating this clearly and distinctly and dealing with the resulting anger, there and then, than you are implying that there might be some hope, and then having to deal with the ensuing disappointment. Honesty will also protect your credibility.

Thank the Group Members for Their Forbearance

A simple statement that you appreciate the group members' willingness to assist and comply in spite of the fact that they may not truly support the change will help to ease their psychological distress. Let the employees know the following:

- It's all right for them not to like everything about the change.
- Management and the change leader respect the diversity of viewpoints and appreciate the cooperation.
- In the interest of continuous improvement, they are encouraged to study the effects of the change and to suggest improvements in appropriate ways.

Keep this meeting as short as possible without rushing it. Devoting more time than is essential may give a message of undue importance and raise unnecessary difficulties. For example, repeating, "I'm really concerned about how you all are feeling about this change" easily could give an unintended but clear message to the employees that they are nowhere near as worried about this change as they should be. Additionally, the longer and deeper you delve into unimportant details surrounding the change, the more important they become in the eyes of those who have to live with the change.

S4: Internal and Nonnegotiable

As is mentioned earlier, internal and nonnegotiable change is rare in the work setting. It is most likely to arise when dealing with internal norms or extreme situations that are out of the ordinary. The paradox is that as rare as we anticipate this to be, it was the only way in which change occurred in work groups prior to the human relations movement. The supervisor—a member of the work group—told the other group members what the change was, and that was it!

Although it is still appropriate for the change leader to initiate and unilaterally insist on a change under extreme circumstances (e.g., stopping dangerous horseplay), S4 generally calls for consensus decision making, particularly in leaderless groups, standing committees, and self-directed work teams.

Describe the Existing Condition or Occurrence and Ask for Responses

The first step is to make sure that everyone in the group is aware of what has happened and what the effects are. For example, "Someone put a dead rat in Phil's locker. Not only is this mean-spirited and childish, it is unsanitary. Upper management, although not reacting yet, is really upset about this. I think we need to deal with this ourselves."

Encourage Discussion

The discussion phase is critical. It is likely that there will be a wide range of opinion about how important the occurrence is. The important thing is that everyone must have an opportunity to talk about it openly. This will increase commitment to the discussion and the eventual outcome.

Obtain Consensus on the Group's Perception

In striving to reach consensus, remember that there doesn't have to be agreement on how important the issue is, only that it is important and needs to be addressed. For example, the leader might say, "Although I do understand that some of you think the trick played on Phil was funny, I am hoping that you also are aware of what the impact of something like this can be in terms of how we are seen as a work group." If consensus is not attainable, you can impose your will or consult with the informal leaders of the group to find out what else may be going on.

Obtain Consensus on the Remedy

It is important that the group members agree that similar behaviors or conditions would not be acceptable in the future. If it is a noninterpersonal issue (e.g., finding a way to respond to a new safety problem), having a subgroup work on a solution or action plan would be appropriate. If the issue in interpersonal (e.g., the trick played on Phil or bullying behavior), and if the group members do not agree that it is unacceptable, the change leader must tell the group members that it must stop.

Develop Consensus on the Penalty for Infraction

Since the objective of this change is to stop something from occurring that would threaten the group or its members, it is important that a suitable and uniform deterrent for future behavior be agreed on. For example, "Any future infractor will be subject to an immediate three-day layoff." This is best determined by group consensus, for several reasons. First, it increases ownership and commitment; second, it helps to ensure a minimum penalty, which is all that is needed to keep the behavior in line.

Unless the infraction is extreme, there should be no penalty for the original incident, because no clear rule was broken. Also, you don't want to make a martyr out of the infractor.

Make Sure That Everyone Is Informed

As change leader, you are responsible for making sure that everyone in the group is informed of the change and that anyone outside the group who would be affected by the change be informed as well.

CONDUCTING THE CHANGE MEETING

Change meetings are as varied as the changes themselves. Furthermore, each meeting for dealing with a specific change is different because the change is in a different stage of development each time. It is best not to have a fixed process in mind, but to have a basic meeting plan in mind—one that can be modified to fit each situation.

Regardless of the nature of the change or its complexity, most change meetings contain the following eight elements:

- Negotiating or acknowledging the contract,
- Establishing the agenda,
- Assigning roles and responsibilities,
- Recording completed actions,
- Implementing the change,
- Developing action plans,
- Determining the next step, and
- Critiquing the meeting.

Acknowledging the Contract

Chapter 4 deals with the purpose and negotiation of the change contract. The contract between the change leader and the group members needs to be established as the first step of every meeting. In the first meeting on the change, the contract is negotiated. In a series of meetings dealing with a specific change, the existing contract is acknowledged at the beginning of each meeting.

Acknowledging the contract is a simple but essential process. It assures that everyone responds to current conditions. All the change leader does is display the contract on a flip-chart poster or overhead transparency, give everyone a moment or two to check it, and then ask if it is all right or whether anyone wishes to suggest changes.

At this time, problems in how the group is working can be reviewed. Any changes in decision making, conflict management, or other processes can be discussed. This is also the best time to change any elements of the current meeting, if necessary, e.g., a need to end the meeting early because of another meeting that several members have to attend.

Establishing the Agenda

The change leader should take a moment to state what he or she hopes will be accomplished at the meeting. The group members should already have the agenda for the meeting; however, one person's expectation might be different from the rest. In some cases a more pressing need may have to be addressed, rather than—or in addition to—the change that the group was dealing with.

Assigning Roles and Responsibilities

The more that individual members can be brought into the process of the change meeting, the more involvement and commitment they develop. Some of the roles that the change leader may want to assign are as follows:

Meeting Leader: The responsibilities of the meeting leader are to see that the agenda is followed and to identify important decisions, action steps, and responsibilities. This role can rotate so that each member has an opportunity to develop meeting-leadership skills, as well as to experience the influence and the frustration that comes with leading a group toward a mutual objective.

Process Facilitator: The process facilitator's role is to focus on how well the group members are working together as they address the change. The process facilitator's responsibilities are to keep communication open and flowing, to refocus the group if it begins to drift away from the topic, and to identify conflict and hidden agendas. The process facilitator does not become involved in the content of discussions, but notes the group's interpersonal processes. The process facilitator may be instructed to interrupt if things are not going well or may be told to hold his or her observations until the end of the meeting and then provide feedback. The role of process facilitator can be assigned to an experienced group member or it can be rotated to help each group member develop process-observation skills.

Gadfly: The gadfly's responsibility, discussed in Chapter 3, is to provide balance in the meeting. The gadfly's job is to point out what might be wrong with what the group is currently doing, to present the opposing viewpoint. This is similar to the role of "devil's advocate."

Recorder: The responsibility of the group's recorder is to take notes on the workings of the group as it deals with the change. The recorder makes lists on flip-chart paper and hangs the sheets on the wall as the group works. Despite common practice, one person cannot serve effectively as leader and group recorder at the same time.

Action Register: This role can be assumed by the group's recorder or it can be held by a separate individual, depending on the number of people in the group, the nature of the task, and the change leader's preference. The responsibility of the action register is to record any assignments to be completed outside the group meeting by group members. The action register records what the action is that is to be completed, who has primary responsibility for it, and by when it is to be done.

Recording Completed Actions

After roles have been assigned, the next step is to obtain reports on any actions that have been completed since the last meeting. If an action has not been accomplished, it is important for the group to know why it was not and then to make any necessary modifications. It is at this stage of the meeting that the group's progress in implementing the change is established.

Implementing the Change

Work on the change continues. The details depend on which of the four change strategies has been selected and how far the implementation has progressed.

Developing Action Plans

As the last piece of working business for the meeting, new action plans are developed. An action plan covers whatever needs to be done outside the group meeting to effectively implement the change.

The action register keeps an ongoing record of the action plans as they are developed and completed. This provides the group with awareness and control of the change process. It also helps the group to maintain a record of its effectiveness so that it can continue with what it is doing or make necessary modifications in how it is implementing the change.

The action plan includes: the intended action, stated in clear, specific, behavioral terms; the person who has prime responsibility for completing the action; the date the action was started; and the date the action is to be completed. The action register also notes the date that the action actually was completed.

A typical action plan would look like the example that follows.

Action	By Whom	Start Date	Planned Completion Date	Actual Completion Date	Other

Typical Action Plan

Determining the Next Step

After the meeting's work has been completed, the change leader gives a summary of what was accomplished in the meeting and indicates what the next logical step is in the implementation. This is always open for discussion, and when completed to everyone's satisfaction, provides the basic agenda for the next meeting.

Critiquing the Meeting

The last order of business of the change meeting is to critique the meeting itself. This can be done in several ways. First, the process facilitator can state what he or she saw in terms of how the group members worked together, noting what needs to be modified. After the process facilitator has provided this input, the group takes a little time to process the information and to acknowledge any needed changes in its behavior.

The second means of critiquing the meeting is to have each member fill out a brief evaluation sheet on the meeting. The change leader collects these and then ends the meeting. Later, the change leader summarizes the information from the evaluation sheets and prepares a summary of the results. This summary is then given to the group members early in the next meeting, so that the members can react to the information and make any necessary adjustments.

A typical evaluation form follows.

MEETING EVALUATION FORM

Date:

Please answer the following questions referring to how effective this meeting has been.

1 = least effective; 5 = most effective.

1. Did the meeting accomplish what was intended?	1	2	3	4	5
2. Was there a clear agenda?	1	2	3	4	5
3. Was the agenda followed?	1	2	3	4	5
4. Were communications open?	1	2	3	4	5
5. Was the meeting leadership effective?	1	2	3	4	5
6. Did the group strive for consensus?	1	2	3	4	5
7. Was conflict productive?	1	2	3	4	5
8. Did the meeting stay on schedule?	1	2	3	4	5
9. Was the level of participation appropriate?	1	2	3	4	5
10. Any additional comments?					

Although taking the time to process the group's interactions adds a few extra minutes to each meeting, it is an investment of time rather than a cost. A few minutes invested in identifying process issues, as a regular part of each meeting, ensures that everyone is aware of what is happening most of the time. A few minutes here can literally save hours of frustration later from mixed or missed communication and unstated disagreements and conflicts.

TIPS FOR BETTER MEETINGS

The following suggestions may help you to conduct more effective and involving change meetings.

Seating Arrangements

How people are arranged in relation to one another has a surprising amount of impact on how they interact with one another. If possible, use a round table, with people sitting equidistant from one another. This will all but eliminate any primacy derived from someone (mainly you) being seated at the "head of the table."

If you are forced to use an oblong table, seat yourself somewhere off-center, on one side of the table rather than at an end, unless you wish to maintain primacy and control with this particular group.

Change Meetings Should Occur on Company Time

Although organizational policy or needs will determine when change meetings occur, it is much better to conduct them during a scheduled part of a regular work day. This is for two reasons. First, it sends a clear message that the organization recognizes that implementing necessary changes is as valued an area of competence and responsibility as is the employee's regular job. Second, if group members are asked to "volunteer" their after-hours time to projects such as change implementation, it will generate more resentment than cooperation. If work on the change must be done outside the regular work day, make sure that overtime or compensatory time is available to cover the time spent.

Logistics

The change leader should attempt to make the work environment as comfortable and informal as possible. The more casual and nonthreatening the surroundings, the higher the probability that people will be willing to interact openly.

Meetings should not be interrupted with messages for group members, except in emergencies. Messages can be taped to the door so that members can respond during breaks.

It is nice to have coffee available during the meeting, if that is consistent with the organization's norms.

Try to work in a room where it is permissible to hang flipchart sheets from the walls. Such sheets are particularly helpful when the group is in the implementing stage and needs to stay in touch with the work it is doing.

CONCLUSION

The intent of this book is to give you a broader view of the change process from the perspective of the individual. Most approaches to change suggest that it is a complex, systems-based strategy. I want to stress that regardless of the issue at hand, change—just like any other organizational variable— gets done by one person talking to another person. The more you can maintain this perspective, the more power you will have in initiating and responding to the change that is occurring in today's organizations.

CHANGE-LEADER ACTIVITY: MEETING PLANNER

Directions: Think about a current or anticipated change that your group is facing. Using the form below, plan the meeting. If there is no change that you can presently react to, choose a change situation from the past that did not go as well as you would have liked. Use the form to describe what you would do differently in order to make it more effective.

1. Purpose of Meeting/Change To Be Discussed:

2. Who Should Attend?

3. Who Should Be Excluded? Why?

4. Where Will the Meeting Be Held?

5. Starting Time:

   Ending Time:

6. What Resources Will Be Needed?

____ VCR player and television

____ Personal computer and presentation monitor

____ Overhead projector and screen

____ Flipcharts and easels

____ Felt-tipped markers

____ Masking tape

____ Paper and pencils

____ Other

7. Who Else Should Be Notified of This Meeting?

8. What Is the Agenda?

CHANGE-LEADER ACTIVITY: LEARNING FROM THE PAST

Concept/Objectives

Although effective change implementation is highly dependent on your ability to work in the present, both past experience and a capacity for visionary thinking are helpful background elements. That is, _learning_ from the past and _planning_ for the future are both here-and-now activities.

One way to develop an effective plan for change is to draw on your past experience as a basis for planning the present change.

Directions:

1. Describe the worst change effort you were ever involved with. Be specific about what the change was and what the results were.

2. What specifically went wrong?

3. What would you do differently with each of the elements from the above list?

4. Describe the best change effort that you were ever involved with. Again, be specific about what the change was and what the results were.

5. What were the specific elements that made it so effective?

6. Describe the proposed change.

7. Based on the above lists, what do you need to be aware of in order to make the proposed change a success?

Answers to Activity Questions

Answers to power analyzer

1. D
2. D
3. D
4. D
5. D
6. A
7. D
8. A
9. A
10. D

Answers to Change-Leader Analyzer (CHAPTER**TWO**)

1. Participative
2. Autocratic
3. Participative
4. Autocratic
5. Participative
6. Supportive
7. Laissez Faire
8. Supportive

Index

Guarantees, demanding, 17
Guilt trips, as a form of resistance, 121-122

H

"Holding the chalk," 62-63
Honoring Your Guilt activity, 170-171
Human capabilities, 14-15
Human inertia, 9
Human resource development, 163

I

Idea generation.
    See Brainstorming
Identification strategies, 98-103
    cause-and-effect analysis, 101-103
    force-field analysis, 98-101
Impacts, identifying, 185
Impasse, in the change process, 41-42
Implementation steps, determining, 192
Individual differences, legitimacy of, 80
Individuals
    announcing change to, 63
    importance of, 55
Inertia, 9
Influence styles, 50
Informal leaders, announcing change to, 63
Information, resistance as a source of, 113-114
Infraction penalties, consensus on, 188-189
Internal negotiable change, 180
    strategy for, 184-185
Internal nonnegotiable change, 181
    strategy for, 187-189
Interpersonal dynamics, of groups, 61
Involvement
    contracts and, 79
    employee, 160
    group, 183, 184-185
    techniques for gaining, 90-103

Involvement-commitment relationship, 61-62
Ishikawa diagram, 101-102
Issues
    addressing and tabling, 80
    focus on, 142
"I" statements, 142
"I won't " statements, 15

J

Judgments, triage method for making, 97-98

K

Key people, negotiating styles of, 138-139
KISS (keep it simple, stupid) criterion, 56

L

Laissez-faire leadership style, 46
Law of Complexity, 178
Law of Distance, 177-178
Law of Enlightened Self-Interest, 18-19
Learning from the Past activity, 198-199
Lewin, Kurt, 98
Listening
    active, 122-123
    empathic, 161-162
    importance of, 117
Loyalty response, 54

M

Majority rule decision making, 93
Management philosophy, 159
Meeting Evaluation form, 193
Meeting leader, 190.
    See also Change leader
Meeting Planner activity, 196-197
Meetings. See Change meetings
Mentoring relationships, 164
Minority rule decision making, 93